THE FRUSTRATION FACTOR

THE FRUSTRATION FACTOR

How To Manage People
Who Drive You Up The Wall

Gary A. Crow, Ph.D.

Glenbridge Publishing Ltd.

Library of Congress Catalog Card Number: LC-94-79174

International Standard Book Number: 0-944435-30-0

Printed in the U.S.A.

TO
E. Allen Finchum

Contents

INTRODUCTION

OVERVIEW

Do you ever have to work with people who absolutely, totally, and unequivocally drive you up the wall? Do you sometimes feel like climbing the wall all by yourself as the quickest way to escape from those people? Are there those days when you struggle with the nearly irresistible impulse to turn into a ranting, raving maniac? Is there that one person who gets you so uptight that you don't know whether to throw your office key in his face and walk out or just sit down and cry? If you are saying **Yes! Yes! Yes!** you have had firsthand experience with "The Frustration Factor," up close and personal.

If instead, these questions are hard for you or if you have never experienced "The Frustration Factor," it is likely that you have lived your life on a very lonely island or are a saint, complete with robe and halo. The Frustration Factor is an ever-present ingredient of organizations from banks to hospitals, from schools to used car dealerships, from large corporations to service clubs.

The dysfunctional behavior of people who drive you up the wall is self-reinforcing and self-perpetuating. It feeds on itself. Unless you are aware of the behavior patterns of the people I call "players" and are prepared to counter them, it is easy to become the foil for their antics. Once this happens, it is too late for most people. The game is on. The world quickly divides into players and foils.

Here is the real problem, though. Anyone new coming into your company enters in the middle of the game. He is immediately part of the process, either as a player or as the foil for other players. The game quickly consumes senseless amounts of time, energy, and company resources. The Frustration Factor becomes a major resource drain. Playing the game takes on as much importance and sometimes more importance for the players than taking care of business.

The Frustration Factor is much the same as the virus causing the common cold. The symptoms are always about the same although the virus has a hundred varieties. Players range from warriors to mainliners, from troublemakers to those who play B-t-B—By the Book. There are players who are aggressive and those who are passive, players who are extroverts and those who are introverts. This book describes and discusses all types of players and their techniques in detail.

PLAYERS IN A NUTSHELL

Players are motivated more by personal needs, status goals, insecurities, and craving for power than by the goals and interests of your company. Dyed-in-the-wool players do not see your company's goals and interests as linked to theirs. The source of their motivation is found in self-promotion, protection, and the acquisition and maintenance of personal power. If their private goals are coincidentally compatible with your company's, so be it. If not, their selfish interests prevail.

Some experienced players are very clever at hiding their motivations, and most all profess to be interested only in the welfare and well-being of your company. They are masters at diverting attention from them and from their roles in the negative outcomes they cause. They are able to displace responsibility onto other people, uncontrollable conditions, and unusual situations. If there is no avoiding responsibility, there are always extenuating circumstances outside the group or organization that make the outcome unavoidable. The result is that the player goes undetected or ends up having people feel sorry for him. It is a pure form of win if you win and win if you lose. No wonder some people become zealous players, all the time, on purpose.

Here is the point you must not miss. Players come in many varieties, and their styles of play range from the subtle to the blatant. In the chapters that follow, players are divided into neat categories and well-defined types. This enables you to clearly see how their techniques and maneuvers work. Be forewarned, though. Experienced players do not restrict themselves to such tidy pigeonholes. They use strategies and approaches from any category that serves their purposes at the time. Skilled play is very creative and original. Whatever their approach to driving you up the wall, please understand that players are very skilled at the game and deserve your respect if not your admiration. If you ever lose sight of this fact, you will be pulled into their games and find yourself driven up the wall over and over again. Your way out of their traps is through learning more about their play and getting equally skilled at counter play.

THE PLAN

Each chapter has four sections. The first is an illustration of skilled players in action. Meetings fall apart, social interactions become heated, and straightforward projects become convoluted and complicated. The settings for these encounters range from corporate conference rooms to elementary schools, from mental health centers to hospitals, from the trivial to the important. The thread they share is the presence and performances of experienced players. The second section of each chapter discusses the illustration, highlighting the words and actions of the players.

The third sections examine the principles of expert play introduced in the chapter. These sections develop the finer points of how players drive you up the wall.

The last sections of the chapters present tips and strategies for effective counter play. You learn specifically how to manage people who drive you up the wall. Understanding effective counter play helps you avoid the traps and snares of the skilled player.

The final chapter moves away from the approach of earlier chapters. It deals with players in negotiations and represents the best and the worst of worlds for you. The payoffs for effective counter play are impressive; the risks of being taken in and driven up the wall are severe. Negotiations with card-carrying players take you into an arena only for those well-schooled in effective counter play. By the time you get to that arena, you are ready. Your task now is to learn how to manage people who drive you up the wall, how to be a skilled counter player.

Chapter One

B-t-B—By the Book

ILLUSTRATION

The operating problems and employee conflicts are festering and have been growing for several weeks. Steve Brown is the assistant manager of the Southland Discount City Store and has avoided any repercussions from downtown so far. But things are getting out of hand.

Besides various other duties, Steve works closely with the cash activities where most of the problems and conflicts are. The difficulties relate generally to scheduling and assignment of employees and to a somewhat higher than usual error rate at the check-out registers. These problems are affecting employee attitudes, and the number of customer complaints is increasing.

"This thing is getting contagious," Steve says in response to the store manager's question. "I have followed the book to the letter on this one and it is not improving. It worries me but I don't know what else to do. If it were up to me, I'd sit them down and tell them the facts of life. It would either straighten up or we would have some new faces around here. It is not my call, though. I think we should give it a little more time. Maybe it will settle down without our doing anything drastic."

The manager leans back in his chair and says, "Steve, the issue is what you are going to do about the problem."

In a sincere voice, Steve says, "Given everything involved, I am bumping this one up to you." Handing a paper to the manager, Steve continues, "Here is the thing in a nutshell. The policy book says to send a problem like this up the line. Here is the I-R-627 on the thing. I have been as complete as I can. I think we better play it safe with this one."

The manager glances at the form but does not read it. Instead, he says, "I still want to know what you are going to do about the problem."

Steve has a frustrated expression as he collects his thoughts and says, "I want to help you out with this one, but it is out of my area. It needs to be handled either by Personnel or the training types. I think it is important for the store for me to stay within my authority. People getting outside their areas is a problem you have, as you know better than any of us."

With only a little more intensity, the manager says, "It will help me if we handle this in-house. Why don't you take this one by the horns and shake it a little? If you get any flack from downtown, I will take care of it for you."

Steve thinks a long time before he says, "I wish I could. I have played this one by the numbers and can't afford to run the chance of its blowing up on me. I don't want to end up the goat."

The manager's frustration now shows. "Steve, I asked you nicely to take care of this problem. Are you going to force me to write this up? If that happens, it will go downtown, and there is no predicting what will come of that."

Steve is slow to respond. "I don't want that any more than you do. It won't help taking the thing out on each other. Give me a couple days to work on it. There has to be some way I can help you get this little thing worked out. It is just not that big of a deal. Let me get back to you on this one."

DISCUSSION

Along with his expertise with the B-t-B method, Steve adds a couple of advanced twists. Note first that he is not one to jump into the middle of things. "The operating problems and employee conflicts are festering and have been growing for several weeks." Ignoring the problem and hoping it will go away is always the first gambit of the B-t-B player. If it goes away, the player takes full credit for the resolution of a difficult problem. If not, he has a chance to come up with a plan to distance himself from it. If luck is truly with him, the player also distances himself from everyone who has even a remote connection to the problem.

"This thing is getting contagious." Steve defines the thing as something going around like the common cold. It is like an act of God or something. Using the phrase "this thing" is good too. It makes a serious operating problem sound like a minor and inanimate object. It is a small step to make it a ball or hot potato to pass around. Then all he has to do is toss it to the manager.

Before tossing the hot potato, Steve makes sure the manager knows Steve has himself covered—By-the-Book of course. His words are worth repeating to emphasize the complex gambit hidden in what seems straightforward. B-t-B players are masters at bundling their play.

"I have followed the book to the letter on this one . . . It worries me . . . I think we should give it a little more time. Maybe it will settle down without our doing anything drastic."

Cover one is going on the record as having followed the book. This puts the responsibility back onto whomever wrote the book.

Cover two is making it clear that Steve worries and feels concerned. This makes him a good company man who is losing sleep over his responsibilities.

Cover three is the best one of all. He makes a concrete recommendation. "I think we should give it a little more time."

Steve suggests doing nothing. This was his plan when he let the problem fester for a few weeks. At least no one will accuse this B-t-B player of being impulsive.

Steve passes off the hot potato in a way that is hardly noticeable. "It is not my call, though;"—another By-the-Book maneuver. He passes it off just as coolly and matter-of-factly as you will ever see. Having made the pass, he confirms the transfer. "Given everything involved, I am bumping this one up to you." The thing is so complex— everything involved —that Steve has to bump it up. The trick is that he only confirms what he did earlier. The B-t-B player first puts the rabbit into the hat and then magically pulls it out.

Steve is close to overkill with, "Here is the I-R-627 on the thing." It is possible for even experienced players like Steve to go too far. If he gets carried away, people can get the impression that he is not a team player.

Steve certainly gets up a head of steam. Listen to him. "People getting outside their areas is a problem you have, as you know better than any of us." Steve is now pointing out problems the manager has in managing people. He likely is even ready to cite chapter and verse. The trap is closed. If the manager insists that Steve deals with the problems in the cash area, he is proving Steve's point. He either deals with the cash problem himself or agrees he is a bad manager or at least not following company procedure. Either way, Steve wins.

The manager sees the trap and shows Steve that he knows a thing or two about effective counter play. His first pass at the B-t-B player is to convince Steve that a cover is unnecessary. More exactly, he offers to cover for Steve if that becomes necessary. "If you get any flack from down-town, I will take care of it for you." Good try! No cigar this time, though.

Steve already has himself covered. He does not need to get on the hook by letting the manager take care of him. "I have played this one by the numbers and can't afford to run the chance of its blowing up on me." In essence, Steve says, "I won't take a chance on you."

Now it is clear why the manager is a manager. "Are you going to force me to write this up? If that happens, it will go downtown. There is no predicting what will come of that."

What does the manager do? He shows Steve he knows a trick or two himself. If he writes it up, it will not bode well for Steve. The manager says that if Steve forces him to play B-t-B, he will. If so, Steve will lose his cover.

Seeing that the manager has him outplayed, Steve goes back to the drawing board. "Give me a couple of days to work on it. . . . It is not that big of a deal. Let me get back to you on this one." Good move, Steve! Do not deal with problems in an impulsive or quick way. Always put it off whenever possible. This gives you time to come up with a new cover.

IN BRIEF (B-t-B)

B-t-B players are slow to deal with problems or conflicts

Once you understand the motivations behind the technique, its use becomes straightforward. First, if the player starts to deal with the issue, he is accepting some degree of responsibility for it. Next, others may hold him accountable for the existence of the difficulties or at least for how things turn out. Playing B-t-B requires someone or something on which to dump the responsibility and the blame if things go sour. For the player dealing with anything lessens his ability to *point the finger* anywhere but toward himself.

B-t-B players play it safe

Using this technique is not as easy as you might first think. The trick is to see that it is a very complex play. First, the player must be able to see when there is a risk of any kind. Next, the successful player uses all his options.

Option one is to avoid doing anything that could turn out badly. Option two is to have a backup or a cut-and-run plan.

Rich is another master with the technique. His main play is to do things the same way he always does them. What has worked before is likely to work again. He knows people seldom find fault with his handling things in the usual way, whether it works or not.

Next, Rich always looks at how things can go sour and little at how they can succeed. He asks, "What are the three strongest reasons for not doing this?" His motto is *nothing ventured, nothing lost.*

Finally, any time he has to do something that has some risk, he spends most of his time figuring out what to say if it goes sour. Of course, the best thing to be able to say is, "I was uneasy about this but went along reluctantly. I handled it the same way we always handle things. I did it *By the Book.* I can only say I held up my end. Someone dropped the ball."

Rich's play calls for doing things the same way he always does them. He avoids all risk as much as possible and has an explanation for failure made up ahead of time. Sure, there is a more simple version of Rich's play. Do not do anything new or innovative and try hard to keep others from making that mistake. When in doubt, do nothing and there is always room for doubt. B-t-B players put most time and energy into worrying and keeping things the same.

For the B-t-B player, any change is a risky business. Any time there is change, there is some degree of uncertainty. This uncertainty makes it unclear how to cover one's self and could require some change in the game plan. For the B-t-B player, the old ways are always the best ways because they are familiar and usually work. Risk to the player is minimal—the player's bottom line. Any change is risky and must be avoided.

B-t-B players never do anything quickly

Timing is everything. For the successful player, timing is the only thing. Those who are aspiring but not yet accomplished B-t-B players think timing has to do with making the right move at the right time. The experienced player knows better. Timing has to do with nothing but not making the wrong move. Better safe than sorry is the motto of the expert B-t-B player. It is a simple truth that one seldom receives criticism for what he does not do. It is also true that things usually work out in a nonnegative way so long as no one interferes. It does not matter what positive outcomes have been precluded so long as things do not get worse. Put this wisdom together and you can easily see why the player figures that it is best to put off decisions and actions as long as possible. The logic is sound. You only need to accept the premise that calls for the safety and no-risk life of the B-t-B player.

The key to using the technique is knowing how to postpone everything. Having a few tricks will be helpful. Here are some things to say if push comes to shove:

- Let me get back to you on this one

- Get me some more hard data

- Give me a couple of days to give this one a closer look

- Better safe than sorry

- This may seem like a little project, but I think your being involved makes it important enough to go slowly

If the pressure builds up, taking it up the ladder, taking it to a staff meeting, or requesting a written recommendation are useful. If it is already in writing, the player asks for a summary or a more detailed proposal, depending on what is not readily available. The goal is to put the whole thing off as long as possible without seeming to be resistive or less than supportive. Many times, everyone just gives up before having to jump through the hoops.

There is a story about a government type who always asks for written requests. The eager staffers prepare their requests in a few days. The day after they turn them in, the bureaucrat gives the requests back with a demand for more data. This process cycles at least three times. At that point, he reads the proposals. The next step is for him to edit the paperwork and give it back to the staffers. This cycles for two or three rounds and then he refers the proposal to either a staff meeting or up the ladder. From there, the game goes on until the staffers give up, quit, or the idea is out of date. The player's rule is that nothing is so urgent it cannot wait.

B-t-B players avoid responsibility

For these players, not accepting responsibility is axiomatic but let's elaborate. The challenge for the player is not to give his game away. Success in the organization depends on being seen as accepting responsibility. The more responsibility the player's superiors think he accepts, the more likely the player will get promotions and more responsibility.

How can the player get the benefits of accepting responsibility without taking on the liabilities? It is actually fairly easy.

First, the player does everything necessary to get into a position of authority or leadership. At lower levels, this happens by volunteering to head projects, chair committees, or anything else that makes other people responsible to the B-t-B player.

The next trick is to delegate all tasks or decisions to those under the player. If things work out well—and they usually will—the player smiles and gives the credit to those who did the work. Of course, everyone can see that this classy person is quite a manager and is definitely someone who can handle responsibility.

If things do not go well, a fixed B-t-B rule says never blame your subordinates. The skilled player says, "My people gave it all they had. They are a great group. It was just a little beyond their reach this time. They have what it takes, though. They will do nothing but get better." Notice how the B-t-B player stays close but just a little above his people. The failure is not their fault and they will do better next time. Of course, the failure has nothing to do with the player himself. The trick here is to be the leader and not part of those people who are responsible.

Sure, the player will need more people, more resources, and probably a bigger title to get the job done next time. It also is as sure as oil going up the wick that there will be a next time.

B-t-B players take no chances

The FastChip Corporation is a small computer supply business catering to the home computer market. Its location in a large shopping center gives the store a lot of traffic and a high percentage of small cash-and-carry sales. The rest of the sales are in the area of $1,000 to $3,000. These larger sales are hardware.

The store policy is not to sell their display stock. If there is no stock in the back, the customer gets a 5 percent discount and delivery within twenty-four hours. This assures that each customer sees the full line.

On Monday, December 1, the store's policies are a problem. An aircraft manufacturer experiences a power disaster that brings down its computer system. As an interim measure, it sends out for thirty-two PC systems. The disaster makes the need urgent.

Rick, the FastChip manager, receives a personal visit from the manufacturer's buyer. The offer is to buy the twelve systems in stock for 90 percent of the retail price. This would take the systems on display and those in the back.

Rick has a problem. Should he follow the store's policies or make a $17,000 sale? Of course, this is not a problem for a B-t-B player like Rick. His first step is to tell the buyer that it will take until 3 p.m. to get a decision. From 11 a.m. when the offer comes, Rick stews over the decision and tries to contact the owner. At 3:30 p.m. when the buyer calls him, Rick tells the buyer they cannot help out this time.

It is a triple play of sorts. Rick puts off dealing with the issue, worries about it, and then opts to play it safe.

What does the owner say when Rick tells him about the missed deal? Do not be silly! B-t-B players never tell, unless it is on someone else. Even if the owner finds out later, Rick can assure him that he tried to contact him. He also can reference store policy and honestly share how much he worried about and struggled with the decision. B-t-B players are, if nothing else, company people. The worst part is that Rick is sure he made the right decision. Better safe than sorry!

MANAGEMENT TIPS

Playing with B-t-B experts is not a game for the impatient or impulsive. It helps to understand that these players have little faith in their abilities and less faith in their basic grasp or understanding of situations or circumstances. Since they do not believe they can trust their judgments or instincts, they do not take any chances on themselves.

Next, they do not have much ability to anticipate or predict the behavior of others. The idea is that they cannot predict if a specific action will lead to praise or punishment. Usually, they think the likely outcome of following their judgment is punishment.

Somewhat oversimplifying their motivations, B-t-B players do not trust themselves and feel any errors or mistakes will likely lead to something bad happening. Counter play, then, has two prongs: increasing the player's faith in himself and emphasizing positive outcomes.

You can force the player to use his judgment more often. Do this by reacting negatively to problems coming up because the player did not use good judgment. For example, "I cannot believe you passed up a $17,000 sale. There are policies to deal with day-to-day kinds of things, but you are here to use a little judgment. There is always a policy to keep our customers happy. If you are going to work here, I expect you to show some discretion about things. Not everything can be done By the Book." The point is to use negative reinforcement to show that negative outcomes can come from playing B-t-B.

Although the negative approach is sometimes useful, as a general rule, a positive approach is better.

Using the same example, suppose the employee reaches the owner. The owner says, "What do you think? Should we do this?" The employee may say "Yes" in some situations or "No" in others, depending on what he thinks is safest. Whatever the player says, the question is then, "Why would you go that way?" The idea is to walk the B-t-B player through the decision making process. In most situations, the interaction can close with, "You seem to have some ideas about this. Use your best judgment."

When the player starts taking more chances and making decisions, it is important not to be too negative when things do not work out well. Avoid the temptation to second-guess the player. Remember that avoiding negative reactions is why he is playing B-t-B.

As you get more experience as a counter player, you will want to consider another possibility. The most likely explanation is that you are dealing with a real B-t-B player. There is the possibility of another problem, though. You may be seeing a pseudo-B-t-B response caused by your behavior. This condition develops if you do not take the time to praise and positively reinforce associates and subordinates. The only response or reaction people get from you is negative or critical. Since there is no likelihood of reward or positive reinforcement, a reasonable person does the reasonable thing. He puts most energy into avoiding negative reactions. The result is a new B-t-B player.

The conclusion is to consider the possibility that the B-t-B player across your desk is a product of your negative behavior. Importantly, though, whether you created or inherited the player from someone else, positive and productive counter play is the same. Teach and encourage in positive and supportive ways. The reward for the player has to come primarily through success and increasing judgment and initiative.

Chapter Two

Faultfinders

ILLUSTRATION

Carol Markowski, principal of Lake Run Elementary School, is making her morning rounds to be sure her staff and students are in their classrooms and working. She will repeat the process this afternoon, knowing that only through her constant vigilance can things run smoothly. Her reputation as a strict disciplinarian is a source of pride to her.

As she makes her inspection, she cannot help wondering to herself, "What is the world coming to?" Her teachers are as bad as the students, from her perspective. "There is probably no hope for any of them," she thinks as she stops to observe a classroom through the window in the door.

As it turns out, her lack of faith receives support. Her attention turns to a half dozen or so sixth graders who are standing around a table in the back corner of the room, doing something. Mostly, it looks like they are only fooling around. This is not the first thing to register with her, though. The two boys at the end of the table look to Carol like they are trouble looking for a place to happen. She just shakes her head, thinking, "It's understandable why education is going downhill when I have to deal with people like that."

As her gaze covers the room, the main problem quickly registers. "Where is Henry Allen," the teacher?

Almost in the middle of her thought, Henry interrupts, "Hi Mrs. Markowski. Are the troops working on their projects?"

Mrs. Markowski asks, "Why are you not in your classroom? It looks like your class is taking full advantage of your absence."

Henry steps closer so he can see through the window. Glancing back at the principal, he says, "They are in groups working on projects they came up with themselves. The deal is that they can work on whatever they want so long as they keep working and cooperating. I don't even know what the projects are. We were talking about accepting responsibility. I stepped out of the room to give them a little experience working together without someone looking over their shoulders."

Mrs. Markowski turns to face Henry. Her voice is low enough to communicate only with Henry but cutting enough to convey her unspoken message. "I have no idea what they are teaching in the colleges these days, but it is surely not about children. You are here to teach them and running around the halls is not teaching. I think you and I better go over your lesson plans for the month so I can give you some instruction in teaching. This will have to get straightened out before your contract comes up in three months. Please be in my office immediately after school." Giving Henry no opportunity to respond, the principal turns and walks down the hallway, continuing her inspection.

Henry watches her walk off and slowly shakes his head. She is always a little testy but today is ridiculous, even for her. His impulse is to do something, although he is not sure what. His choices seem even more unprofessional than the principal's behavior. Instead of giving into the impulse to lash back, he shrugs his shoulders and returns to his students.

A couple hours later Henry walks into the teachers' lounge during his free period. Two other teachers, Doris and Greg, are already there.

Doris is saying, "It's their fault down in that office. They always get things fouled up. If I were running this place, a few heads would roll. We work our tails off and they can't get anything right."

Picking up on the assault, Greg says, "Do we ever get a thank you or how do you do? Not a chance! I don't know why our so-called union doesn't do something about that stuff we have to put up with."

Henry, who is also the president of the teachers' union, tries to chalk it up to one of those days. It's just in the air, he thinks. Despite his effort to stay out of it, he reflexively rebuts, "The union can't do it all."

"That union is about worthless," Greg says, turning the attack to Henry.

"The union does many good things for us," Henry replies, trying to put things onto a more positive note.

Doris joins in, "The point is what have you done for us today? The only way we little people get anything is by hitting you big shots over the head with the problems. Just about the time it looks like something is going right, something else gets screwed up."

Henry says, "I think we can be proud of what we have accomplished."

Doris gets herself another cup of coffee as she says, "I'm just not one to get all sloppy about covering up the problems. Give your type a compliment or a little praise and you think you've got it made. That's the last we hear from you. You're as bad as some of those students I have. I'll ask you again. What have you done for us today?"

Not to be outdone, Greg adds his two cents worth. "You've done a few things, Henry. I'll give you that. The problem is what you have not done."

Not waiting to see if Greg had more to say, Henry interrupts. "I'm glad to hear we are at least doing a few things right. What about that basketball team of yours, Greg? I don't think six and nine is anything to brag about. You expect the union to win every time. If anyone held you to that, you'd be out of here."

Greg is hot under the collar now. "If you think you can do any better with that bunch of so-called jocks I have to work with, you're welcome to them."

Ilene Stuart, the special education teacher, comes into the lounge and into the middle of the fracas. Quietly she says, "It sounds like you want blood. I think Greg is doing all right. Those kids are only eleven and twelve and two of them are my kids. With no more experience than Greg has, I think he is doing all right. That goes for Henry too. He's a teacher and can't be expected to know anything about running a union. It's what we all have to put up with around here. We all have to take on things we don't know anything about. It's not our fault things are in such a mess."

Doris is quick to come to Ilene's side. "You can say that again. It's about time we start calling them like they are. It's time to put the responsibility directly on the people who are causing the problems. We all know who they are too. It all comes down to the person who did or did not do whatever. It boils down to the person who is responsible, the person who didn't get the job done. It's just a few who make us all look bad and make it impossible for us to do our jobs. We're all good teachers but that doesn't matter around here. We spend all our time trying to straighten out the details, the little things other people haven't taken care of."

Not to be upstaged and feeling like things are turning more to his liking, Henry says, "I know people have bad days but that's no excuse. They have to do it right every time, including the little things. Taking it out on us is intolerable. It is professionalism we are talking about, and the students are the ones to suffer in the long run."

Everyone nods at the profundity. Ilene says, "It's attitude. It is our responsibility to keep things on a positive note, no matter how we feel. I do it and don't see why everyone else can't do it. Henry is right, it is a matter of professionalism."

DISCUSSION

Faultfinders like to throw their weight around, if they have any weight to throw. Carol's criticism of Henry at his classroom door is a classic example and the work of a master player. Mrs. Markowski, in one short burst, puts Henry in the position of student with her as teacher. She threatens to have his contract nonrenewed (we used to call this getting fired). Additionally, she gives him what the students would call an after-school detention. Finally, she lets him know she can and will tear his lesson plans into little bits. Given the opportunity, faultfinders like to get people into trouble—a natural for the school principal. It also is an effective way to put the president of the union in his place while she is at it.

"There is probably no hope for any of them." This tidbit from Carol's thoughts is a telling sign of her qualifications as a faultfinder. She is always ready and willing to be critical of anything and anyone. The successful faultfinder never forgets that the world is full of things and people to analyze and criticize.

Budding faultfinders have made a giant step once they simply assume people are going to screw up sooner or later. It also helps if the eager player believes others are doing it just to give him a bad time.

Doris gives you a good example of the technique. In the middle of saying something else, she says, "It's just a few who are making us all look bad . . . ." The point is that any time Doris looks bad, someone did it to her. This is what advanced faultfinders call a position of perfection. No matter what they do or do not do, they do it well. Any problems are someone else's fault.

The teachers provide many examples of The Frustration Factor. Carol Markowski just shakes her head and thinks, "It's understandable why education is going downhill when you have to deal with people like that."

"People like that" is a key to her success as a player. It is obvious that she puts most people into the category and changes the definition of "like that" as she goes along. She does this even if sometimes the people are only twelve years old. Intolerance and an unwillingness to accept people as is make it much easier to be critical.

For those who elevate faultfinding to an Olympic-class sport, it is necessary to be stingy with praise. Skilled players keep the focus on problems, negatives, and things going wrong. This includes anything from the important to the trivial, from the essential to the irrelevant.

Henry shows you how to use the play with style. He does not even need to have an opening. "I don't think six and nine is anything to brag about." Henry has as much potential as Carol Markowski, given more experience and practice. He comes straight out of left field.

A close look clarifies the technique. Pick something, anything the person may value that is not going well, e.g., Greg's basketball team. Pounce on that since it will hurt, and then stress how it is as bad or worse than the problems the faultfinder is having. "You are worse than I am." That is Henry's point. The underlying game is to play one up even if the player has to admit some shortcomings.

Ilene, the special education teacher, demonstrates a related technique with style. Even her efforts to compliment have a backhanded quality. They are the type of compliment that makes the recipient say, "Thanks, I think."

She says, "With no more experience than Greg has, I think he is doing all right. That goes for Henry, too. He's a teacher and can't be expected to know anything about running a union."

Two phrases tell the tale: With no more experience than Greg has, and he's a teacher and can't be expected to know anything. Her point is that, were Greg more experienced or Henry not just a teacher, they would function more competently. It would not be surprising to see her walk over and pat each of them on the head and say, "It's all right. I know you're trying."

Doris is not to be outdone as a first class faultfinder. "It's time to put the responsibility directly on the people who are causing the problems. We all know who they are, too." It is certain enough to take to the bank that who they are excludes Doris and probably everyone else in the room, unless someone leaves. If someone walks out, they can count on joining Doris's "who they are" group.

Faultfinders seldom pursue their game on a face-to-face basis. Behind-the-back makes it much easier to avoid anyone's directly contesting or rebutting what they have to say.

Henry wraps the faultfinding demonstration up in style. It is no wonder he qualifies as a faultfinder complete with professional credentials. Listen to what he says. "I know people have bad days but that's no excuse. They have to do it right every time." Henry is the keeper of the standard, the last supporter of perfection. From that perspective, it is easy, nay unavoidable for Henry to be anything other than faultfinding. He is just doing what comes naturally for saints like him and Carol Markowski.

IN BRIEF

Faultfinders do not have much faith in people

Management and psychology texts argue that people will do as well as they can under the specific circumstances. They only need to accept the underlying values, understand the problem, and receive support and encouragement. Faultfinders do not buy into that. It is only necessary for them to look around to see the absurdity in the "people-are-good-and-want-to-do-the-right-thing" hypothesis. These players can look at almost any behavior, activity, or project and point out things that should have worked out better or faster. They can point to people who should have been smarter or sharper. They also call attention to events or circumstances that someone should have handled more smoothly or efficiently.

They always do better, they believe, so it is reasonable for them to expect others to do the same. Faultfinders reason thusly:

• If things were done right the first time, we would not have to waste our time straightening out messes other people are causing

• There is no excuse for that—whatever that happens to be

• If you can't do the job, we'll find someone who can—
and that will be easy to do

The trick is to faultfind about something, anything, and
then criticize someone, anyone. The result is that the spotlight never gets turned on the player. If the heat does turn
on him, he only needs to escalate his criticism and self-
righteous indignation.

Faultfinders are intolerant of others

Intolerance is to faultfinding as a lack of reason is to
dogma. Remove the intolerance and this frustrating behavior must stand the test of reality and the close examination
of others. It is this type of scrutiny the player wants to avoid
whenever possible.

The faultfinder is always looking for the different, the
negative, or the problematic in others. If the player shows
any real tolerance, he runs the risk of overlooking these
negative aspects. Attention must not shift to people's
strengths, abilities, or areas of special competence. This is a
risk that must be avoided. Maintaining a high level of intolerance is safe and guarantees there will always be room for
faultfinding.

Faultfinders expect others to foul up

This principle joins with intolerance and the next principle to form a closed triad. Simply expecting others to foul
up enables the player to predict the behavior of people with
one hundred percent accuracy. Sooner or later everyone

will handle something less than perfectly. The player's intolerance makes it easy to see the negative or problematic. Assuming that the foul up will happen leads to his being sharper and quicker to pounce on it.

It is a variant of Murphy's law. Sooner or later things will go wrong, and it is likely to be sooner. When it happens, the player is not surprised. He and Murphy predicted it.

It is easy for the player to spot and respond to what he expects. If everyone thinks a member of the family will foul up, they will be more alert, more on guard, and quicker to blame. When people expect the worst, there is seldom any surprise. Even if things are going well, "Just you wait!"

Faultfinders do not accept people as they are

Now the triad is complete. There is intolerance. There is the expectation others will foul up. Now, however people are, they should change.

The player says, "I do not like the way you handled that project."

The staff member watches the player for a while to see how projects should be handled and then uses the player's approach for the next project.

The faultfinder then says, "I do not like the way you handled this project."

The staff member says, "But it is the same way you do things."

The player then says, "I might have expected you to be someone who would try to take someone else's techniques. You need to be original."

Here is the triad in another context.

Mike works beside Ralph on the assembly line. Mike says, "Ralph, you are going to drive me crazy if you don't stop moving your lips like you are chewing your cud when you operate that press."

Ralph says, "Get off my back!"

Mike comes back with, "You people from the south plant are all alike. I don't know why they put you in here even if we are short on help. We'd be better off without help like that."

Ralph is hot now. "What do you mean by that? If it weren't for us, nothing would ever get finished around here."

Mike lashes back. "I get tired of fixing things you screw up."

"Have I screwed up anything yet?" Ralph asked.

"Not yet, but just give you enough time."

It is a safe bet that Mike's prediction will eventually come true, and he will be ready to pounce.

Faultfinders are stingy with praise

Recall from the Discussion section that giving someone praise is dangerous. It can backfire by encouraging the person to do more that is praiseworthy. The faultfinder does not want this to happen. It gets much harder to find things to faultfind about. It is like a hunter encouraging all the game to leave his favorite hunting ground. Faultfinders tend not to be either stupid or self-defeating.

Faultfinders enjoy blaming and accusing people

The key here is that no one has to be at fault or in a position to be accused of anything. A typical example might go like this.

Karen says to Bill, her office mate, "The truth is it is your fault I didn't get that promotion."

Bill asks, "How do you figure?"

That is the opening Karen is looking for. "You missed your appointment in Atlanta, and the result was your proposal was late."

Bill interrupts, "But I was snowed-in at Cleveland."

Karen responds, "It is always something with you."

Puzzled at the attack, Bill asks, "What does that have to do with your getting or not getting the promotion?" A big mistake, Bill!

Karen is ready. "I would not expect you to understand that kind of political thing. I work with you and you drop the ball. That makes me look bad and I do not get the promotion I deserve."

More attentive now, Bill says, "Let me get this straight. I get snowed-in at Cleveland. My proposal is late, and because of that you end up not getting a promotion."

With a wave of disgust, Karen ends the conversation. "You've got that one right."

Faultfinders focus only on what is not going well

By this point, it is probably clear to you that focusing on the problematic and negative is the stock-and-trade of faultfinders.

"Please type a draft of this letter for me."

A couple of hours later, "I'm getting tired of errors in the things you type for me."

The typist says, "I did it in a hurry. I thought it was a draft and you wanted it in a hurry." Sorry, no win this time.

"I expect that even a draft will not be full of errors. (There were three errors.) You need to remember if something is worth doing, it is worth doing right."

To herself, the typist thinks, "I don't think you would think anything was right."

This is a perceptive typist. The faultfinder will always find fodder for his cannon.

Faultfinders are not proud of the achievements of others

Suppose Karen and Bill both get promotions.

Karen says, "Wow! Don't you think it's great I got that promotion? I've worked hard and deserve it."

Bill says, "It's terrific! I think it's terrific for me too."

Karen responds, "Sure it's nice for you. It isn't that big of a deal for you, though. You're a man so you can expect promotions almost automatically."

Faultfinders expect others to do as well
as they sometimes do

If there is a major player around and especially if he is in a position of authority, it does not pay to be exceptional. For example, a salesman has an unusual week. He hits on almost every call and ends up the week 60 percent over his solid but not outstanding average.

His sales manager says, "I knew you had it in you. You have been holding back on us. This is more like it, more up to your potential. This is the kind of work I'll be expecting from now on. No more of this shirking. You are a great salesman."

Of course, this is like expecting a baseball player to get a hit every time he comes to the plate or your child always to get A's. Nonetheless, it is the stock-in-trade of a first class faultfinder. Their motto is nothing but better will do for everyone else.

Faultfinders place the blame squarely
on the person who did not get the job done

"It is your fault. We were counting on you, and you let us down."

On the surface, this may not seem like a technique for faultfinders. It is best to hold the responsible person directly responsible. The twist is that the faultfinder is literal about this. In the example above, Bill should not have been late with the proposal. He should have known it snows in Cleveland in the winter and made contingency plans. It was his job to get the proposal in on time, and it is his fault that it was late.

The technique is probably becoming clearer to you by now. The idea is that, no matter what, there are never any extenuating circumstances or mitigating conditions. The expectation is absolute and unconditional. Either there is success or there is a person who failed. The trick is for the player to use the technique while avoiding its being used on him.

If the player was the responsible person when things went awry, the best trick is to say, "I did my part. My part of the project went fine. It did not work out because there were several parts that had to be done right. There were a couple of the parts for which I was not responsible that went wrong."

Suppose the project is putting in a new light bulb. Joe is responsible for light bulb replacement. As a first class faultfinder, he says, "It is not as simple as just putting in a new bulb. Nothing around here is so simple. The problem is that John forgot his keys, and I let him use mine. I can't get into the closet without a key. By the time he finally got around to bringing my key back, there was insufficient time to install the fixture. The problem is that there is inadequate coordination of facility access. We have some big problems around here."

MANAGEMENT TIPS

The dynamics of faultfinders are interesting in so far as they are not what you might expect. People trying to deal with these players are apt to see them as confident people who have high standards and a low tolerance for anything less than perfection. The real issue is that they cannot separate the important from the unimportant, the essential from the unessential. They can recognize an exact duplicate of something, know when people are following the rules or tell when things are not right. What they cannot recognize is a reasonable example of something. They cannot tell when someone does a job well enough for the purpose. They cannot see that behavior sometimes only varies in style or as a function of personality. They need an exact match or they see no match at all.

The trick is to look at the faultfinder's behavior or performance. If you see a flaw or problem in the player, he also sees it and amplifies it many times. The player has little faith in himself, has little tolerance for personal shortcomings, and is self-blaming about things that were unavoidable. Faultfinders have a standard to which they compare themselves, and they fall short.

The first step in managing these players is to see that they are not doing anything to others they do not do to themselves. That helps you take their behavior less personally. They are only pointing out a problem or difficulty. The variance from their standard bothers them more than any person in particular, as hard as this may be to see at the time.

Next, faultfinders not only expect others to foul up but also fear they will do so. They are not accepting of others but are not accepting of themselves either. If you watch them, you will see that they treat themselves as critically as they treat others.

This insight leads to the best technique to use with these players. As with anyone who drives you up the wall, do not react, do not come to the bait. The bait is the urge to react negatively, to tell them off, to refuse to work with them, or to resign to the inevitable while you are boiling inside. Instead, make the changes that are appropriate and reasonable. Remember that they are sometimes right and not just faultfinding. The rest of the time, do only what needs to be done, as well as it needs to be done.

Here is the real trick. Without overdoing it, find honest opportunities to say supportive things to these players. Point out things they have done especially well. Comment on it when one of their skills or abilities makes things easier or helps things turn out successfully. Over time, relating to them in these positive ways will modify the way they treat you. It will have little affect on their behavior with other people. The technique only tends to benefit the one who uses it.

As a closing thought, be alert to a special context in which faultfinders do some of their most destructive work. The behavior occurs in casual conversations in hallways, before and after meetings, and when people are not expecting anything important.

The faultfinder makes a comment to you about someone who is not present. The comment just slips into the conversation in a low-key way, appearing to be innocuous.

"I wonder how Linda is doing with that project. She is having more trouble than a kid learning to ride a bicycle. I wish I had time to help her, but you know how it goes."

This player is a sensitive person who only wishes he could do more for Linda and perhaps for the company. Here is a real team player.

As an experienced counter player, you see the real game, though. The faultfinder is running a complex gambit on you. Here are the elements:

- Linda is not doing very well

- Her project is as commonplace as riding a bicycle

- The player could do Linda's project quickly and well, if he had the time

You say something like, "Linda has her hands full. That project is more complex than it seems at a glance. You can be glad you do not have time to get involved."

Your counter play puts the faultfinder on notice. You are not going to play the game at Linda's expense. This is a good thing for your colleagues to know. Further, your counter play shows, in a positive way, the importance of a thorough understanding of what is and is not happening before passing judgment. Finally, you are able to model these positive techniques without falling into the trap of criticizing anyone. When dealing with faultfinders, take care to avoid dealing with the problem by doing a little faultfinding of your own.

Chapter Three

Warriors

ILLUSTRATION

Brent Miller, Research and Development manager of the CAG Corp., is quietly confident. He makes a last minute check of the cable connections and adjusts the focus on the projector. This is the best shot he will get at the funding for the test installation. He spent the last three weeks getting this presentation together and feels confident. This time he has it right. There will be no rerun of January's fiasco.

Last January, his departmental report did not go well. A few people at the management meeting could not see well enough to read his charts. Also, he was a little casual in presenting his data. By the time he finished, everyone felt confused, including Brent. This will not happen this time. Today's presentation is clear, concise, and simple enough for an idiot, he thinks, as the lights dim.

Brent's dog-and-pony show takes twelve minutes, leaving eight of the allotted twenty minutes for a quick question and answer session. When the lights are back up, Brent confidently asks if there are any questions. This is his big mistake.

The other managers take the mandatory few seconds to glance around the paneled room. They are waiting to see if Mark Ross, the Senior Vice President for Operations, goes first. Mark watches Brent but does not say anything.

Ronda Simpson breaks the ice. "That was good, Brent. I understand your data better than I did in January."

For an uneasy moment, Brent wishes he could crawl into the woodwork and disappear. He expected her to say something about his January report but not so quickly and directly. Ronda is usually much more subtle with her little barbs.

Brent is quickly past the urge to hide and ready to fight, if that is what Ronda wants. He smiles and says, "Given your twenty years as a manager, Ronda, I will take that as a compliment."

Let the games begin. The polite atmosphere when the meeting began is over. Ronda bristles and is on the verge of responding to Brent's dig when Harold Stiner, Production manager, jumps in. Somewhat more deliberately than Ronda, Harold says, "I know you have only been with us for a year, Brent. There are a few things you seem to be still struggling with. You want $150,000 to—what did you call it?—place two machines. What you want to do is spend a quarter million once you add the hundred you will need to support your test. Production keeps getting pushed to cut costs, and your boys in R&D want a hundred here and a hundred there. I know you want to be sure, but your price seems a little steep."

More interrupting than responding to Harold, Brent asks, "How much can we handle for this test installation?"

Harold imperceptibly tenses as he responds, "It's Mark's call but as far as I'm concerned, R&D wants to push up the cost unnecessarily. We have two machines on the floor down below, and they work just fine. We only have orders for ten units and this would add twenty-five bills to the cost of each unit shipped. My concern is that this will get the price up so high we'll get stuck with the lot of them."

Ronda smiles at Harold as he handles the new kid on the block and is quick to join sides against Brent. Ronda looks at Brent and fixes him with her famous stare. She delivers her equally famous admonition as if to one of her subordinates. "It may be back to the drawing board, Brent."

Ronda expects Brent to back off, but he does not. Harold works with Brent on a couple other projects and also expects Brent to capitulate. Usually this is exactly what Brent's response is. After all, he is an engineer and not a conference room maneuverer. Not this time, though. This time no one is going to take advantage of his normally passive nature. "I'm going to push on this one. My recommendation is no machines get shipped until R&D is comfortable. That will be tough until I test two in the field. This one is not my call, but there is a real downside risk in any tendency to ignore the hard data."

A sharp squeal no one immediately recognizes snaps the tension in the room. It is Brent's beeper. There is a problem in the lab. Harold and Ronda say something to each other that Brent cannot hear as he awkwardly excuses himself and makes his way past Mark Ross.

Ronda is ready to start her report but the V. P. says, "We will have to do this later, Ronda. They have me on a tight schedule today. Why don't you drop off a copy of your report and my assistant can brief me on anything important?"

DISCUSSION

Being a social scientist or having forty years experience with corporate politics are not necessary to recognize the big league warriors in the conference room. Nonetheless, it is worthwhile to observe people who play with such style and to study the principles underlying their play.

Stepping on the feelings of others is a trademark of warriors. Ronda does an effective job with this technique when she tells Brent, "That was good, Brent. I understand your data better than I did in January."

She steps on his feeling of satisfaction with a good report in which he has invested three weeks and a lot of himself. She also manages to drag up the problems with his report last January. Ronda is not one to let a sleeping dog lie. It seems likely Ronda has a file of past errors and omissions, probably cross-indexed by topic, name, and likely times to drag them back up.

Brent is not to be outdone when it comes to being a warrior. "Given your twenty years as a manager, Ronda, I will take that as a compliment." The part elevating him to the rank of warrior is not this jab alone, though. Looking more closely, Brent is going all out for his plan as he goes for Ronda's throat. While he is at it, he rubs her nose in the fact that she, with her twenty years of experience, is at the same organizational level as he. Brent is showing signs of becoming a real conference room maneuverer.

Harold shows you that he also is no piker when it comes to being a warrior. "As far as I'm concerned, R&D wants to push up the cost unnecessarily. . . . My concern is that this will get the price up so high we'll get stuck with the lot of them."

Harold makes the point succinctly so no one misses his thrust. His lack of any tendency to discuss the issues shows he is inflexible and not one to compromise. This approach is, by itself, enough to qualify Harold as a warrior. But he goes that one or two better. He reminds Brent that he, Brent, is the new kid on the block. He also suggests that Brent and his R&D colleagues would give away the store. People like Brent and his associates do not understand business, from Harold's point of view.

Harold also advances his play in a subtle way. It comes when he refers to Brent's request as unnecessary. The unsaid message is, "If you had done your job right, what you are suggesting would not be necessary." In a somewhat harsh and abrasive way, Harold implies that Brent is not much of an engineer either.

Ronda is not easily outdone in the harsh and abrasive department. "It may be back to the drawing board, Brent." Being a truly skilled warrior, Ronda shoots her dart with humor and a smile, you can be assured.

Brent may eventually outdo both Ronda and Harold in being a skilled warrior. He does this by being sharp enough not to let anyone take advantage of him or his youth. "I'm going to push on this one. . . . There is a real downside risk in any tendency to ignore the hard data." Is Brent telling Harold and Ronda that they are so unsophisticated as to ignore the hard data, if they are aware of and understand such things? Yes, he is. Brent is indeed a player.

What about Mark, the V. P.? Does he qualify as a warrior? A close look shows he is the most destructive player of all. The evidence comes particularly at two points. The first point is when he stays passive and does not assume his proper role in the meeting. At this point, the vice president has a chance to take the lead and avoid the conflict all together. The second point comes when he says to Ronda, "Why don't you just drop off a copy of your report, and my assistant can brief me on anything important." *Anything important*? Mark discounts Ronda and dismisses her. He also makes it clear her report probably contains nothing important and can be handled by his assistant. In the same breath, he also manages to avoid any personal responsibility for the decision. "They have me on a tight schedule today." Mark puts Ronda in her place and dumps the blame onto his subordinates.

IN BRIEF

Warriors never give anyone an inch over anything

- I am a perfectionist

- Either it is right or it is wrong

• Rules are rules

These types of phrases frequently come up when you try to manage warriors. Interestingly, players who use this technique are likely to make their pronouncements when others are around and will overhear. When focusing their play on one person—usually a subordinate—warriors like to be sure others hear so they learn not to test the player. They have been forewarned.

Warriors step on the feelings of others

Since most people are at least a little insecure about their competence and ability to work with others, these players play on others' insecurities. Some phrases from an office environment are instructive.

• That is trash

• More of the same old stuff

• Dragging your feet

• Out of your area of expertise

• Roadblock

• They—followed by any negative pronouncement

Add any other phrase or statement to the list implying that the other person is at fault, incompetent or less skilled and cooperative than the player. The key is to get them where it hurts.

Warriors are ready to go to war over anything

At first glance, these players may seem to be the same as those who never give an inch. Although they are chips off the same block, these players are just as likely to go for the throat for what they want as for what someone else wants. The crux of the technique is drawing blood. These players say things like:

- If you won't go to the mat over the little things, they will just get out of hand

- You either win or you lost

- I enjoy a good fight

- If they want to go to war over this, it is war they've got

After a while, it becomes clear that the war is the thing. Even if they get what they want, they will find something to argue about, hoping to start another war.

Warriors are harsh and abrasive

The essence of this technique is more in the delivery than in the content. Players who have mastered this technique understand that the barb must be short and quick to work well. It is a sharp jab, a well-placed phrase or a quick response.

Ask the player, "Do you have a minute for a quick question?" The instantaneous response is, "No, not right now." Then the player immediately turns his attention away from the person asking the question, if his attention was there to begin with. Mark's exit from the conference room is also a good example of this technique. It is quick, specific, and allows no opportunity for discussion or rebuttal. The key is to hit and run.

The technique comes up in other contexts. For example, the player suddenly has to leave but says something cutting or troublesome on his way out the door. Those still in the room are left to deal with the problem.

Warriors never let anyone take advantage of them

The interesting point here is that these players think people are always trying to take advantage of them. They spend their time and energy figuring out how everything will lead to their getting had. Warriors are to be admired for the levels of energy they put into their game. It takes constant vigilance to be sure no one ever takes advantage of them.

One of their automatic questions is, "Why?"

"Would you like to go to lunch?" "Why?"

"May I use your phone?" "Why?"

"How's it going?" "Why do you ask?"

The player's need is to evaluate *everything* in terms of how he might get had. His motto is, "If I don't take care of myself, no one else is going to do it for me."

Warriors will argue with anyone, anywhere, at any time

This may seem like never giving an inch or always being ready to go to war. To some extent, that is true. The new twist is that these players do not have to win and do not necessarily expect to win.

You ask a worker to move to the office next door. That office is exactly like the one he has and the move is to allow a new handicapped worker to be closer to the outside door. The player says, "I am not going to put up with being pushed around. If you think you can get away with this, you're wrong!"

In another example, two people are talking about something having nothing to do with the player. Nonetheless, he listens for a few seconds and then disagrees with something said. And the argument starts.

The most destructive examples are when an employee argues with a colleague in front of a customer. Remember these players will pursue their advantage anywhere with anyone, even if it is with the customer himself.

Warriors try to take charge of everything and everyone

Warriors who have mastered taking charge are also apt to take charge, give advice, or intrude when people are capable of taking care of things themselves. For example, "If I were you, I'd do that this way." This works especially well when the person receiving the advice neither asks for it nor needs it. This technique also is operating when players try to tell others how to arrange their offices, their schedules, their desks, or their lives, given the opportunity.

An instructive example of the "Take Charge" technique happens during a player's interview for the position of president of a small corporation. Watch and learn.

The player is sitting at the side of the conference table in the board room when his final interview starts. On the first question, he slowly gets up and starts walking toward the front of the room—to the head of the table.

By the third question, he is standing behind the chairman. On the fifth question, he steps back to the flip chart, picks up a pen, and illustrates his answer. While doing this, he asks the chairman to move so others can see better. The chairman moves.

When the player finishes illustrating his point, he moves back behind the chairman's chair. During the answer to the next question, he sits down in the chairman's chair.

This player certainly takes charge—and believe it or not—he gets the job a half hour later.

Warriors expect others to adjust to them, no matter what

A good motto for these players is, It's my way or no way. Brent and Harold model this technique when they lock horns in the conference room. Brent insists on two field tests. Harold is emphatic that there will be no more tests. The key is that both of them seem to feel that getting the other to give in is more important than having a quality product at a competitive price. Each has his idea and point of view and expects the other to capitulate.

This play also comes up in trivial situations. Try to schedule an appointment with a committed warrior.

"I need to talk with you. Can we get together this week?"

The player says, "This week is tight. How about next week?"

"Well, all right. I could make it on Monday or Thursday."

The player says, "No good. Wednesday or Friday is it."

"Well, I could change a couple of things to make it Friday morning."

The player says, "That's out. It will have to be afternoon."

"Well, I am going to take my mother to the doctor at 3:00 so how about 1:30?"

The player says, "No can do. I'll be taking a long lunch that day so won't be available before 3:30."

"Well, I will just have to reschedule with the doctor. 3:30 it is."

The warrior closes the game. He says, "I'll pencil you in. Call me that morning to be sure the time is still open."

Warriors do not believe in being flexible
or accommodating to the needs, preferences
or individual situations of others

This pattern of play is not the same as expecting others to adjust. Here, the player does not push others to adjust or accommodate. Rather, his only rule is not to adjust to or accommodate to other people. The operative motto is, "You do your thing and I'll do mine."

These players religiously refuse to negotiate or horse trade. An alternative motto might be, "If you do not want to play by my rules, I will take my ball and go home." If the other players have a ball of their own, warriors go home anyway.

MANAGEMENT TIPS

Warriors are overly aggressive, insensitive, rigid, and have an unusual need to control people and situations. Understanding these characteristics is the key to effective counter play. Never giving an inch over anything, never letting anyone take advantage of them, and trying to take charge of everything are the essence of their play. When managing these players, first keep in mind that they mistrust everyone and their motives. With this as a given, you can see that they operate mostly out of fear and insecurity and honestly believe keeping absolute control is the only way to be safe.

Next, warriors create a negative and emotionally charged environment for their game. Stepping on the feelings of others and being harsh and abrasive keep others off balance and preclude any personal involvements that might weaken or interfere with their game. It is important for them never to be in a situation where they have to deal with people as people.

Finally, warriors use arguing and a reputation for going to war over everything as a technique to keep others on guard and at arm's length. This fighting posture enables the player to defend his turf and to keep the game away from emotional or "feeling level" tricks. The game is and will remain a matter of who has the most muscle and the greatest willingness to go to the mat over everything.

With this in mind, counter play is not complex. Yes, it is difficult. It requires great patience and skill, but it is not complicated. Warriors are insecure and feel threatened by almost anything. The key is to stay away from the usual technique of trying to get cooperation by showing the other person how cooperation will work to his advantage. With warriors, that is not an incentive to go along. Instead, the skilled counter player says, "If you don't want to go along with me on this, I respect your choice. I thought I might be able to help you avoid the problems you are going to have over this. If they are not of concern to you, I have other things to do."

For example, in the illustration Brent would do better using this technique with Harold than he does by getting into an argument. He can say, "Harold, I see your point about the price and appreciate your concern. Nonetheless, it may be better to test things out now instead of running the risk of your having to deal with irate customers. What do you think?"

As you develop a feel for pointing out negative outcomes to warriors, pulling it off depends on neither arguing nor reacting to hurting comments. No matter how cutting the barb, say, "Thank you for sharing that with me. My point is . . . ." If the player starts to argue over anything—and he will—passively listen until he stops talking. Now say, "My point is . . ." It is an exercise in being thick-skinned. Do not react or respond to the garbage. Assertively and calmly stay on task and on the point.

The rule for managing warriors is not to be intimidated. Also, never come to the bait, no matter how tempting or irresistible. The bait, of course, is the urge to defend your-self, attack the warrior, become totally frustrated, and quit or simply capitulate to his will.

It will help to think in terms of a strong vacuum into which you can be pulled. The aggressiveness and nerve of the player causes what psychologists call a fight/flight response. There is an urge to strike out on the one hand and a competing urge to avoid warriors all together on the other hand. Interestingly, either response serves their purposes. As a skilled counter player, you will find your purpose best served by doing neither.

How do you do neither? The trick is to understand that what you are feeling is inside you. It is not inside the war-rior. The player only has the level of power to affect you that you give to him.

For example, if you are dealing with a warrior and if you feel the fight/flight urge, you need to understand that the conflict is within you. It is not between you and the player. It is your problem.

Once you catch on to the problem within you, you take back your power. Now you need neither fight nor flee. You do not need to stand your ground either. That is the same as getting ready to fight.

Your goal is to disempower warriors. This happens by doing nothing. Listen if you are interested or have no choice but,

• Do not let the player affect your behavior or actions

• Do not get pulled into conflict or confrontation

• Do not knowingly do anything that gives the player any more power

If the situation becomes desperate, think about something else, do not pay attention and mentally back away for awhile. Better to be accused of not being attentive than to fall into the player's trap.

Chapter Four

Bummed Out

ILLUSTRATION

Maryanne Mitchell is the office manager for the Koch, James, and Hightower law firm. She is meeting with Martin Koch. It is not unusual for Martin to ask her to stop by, but still she gets up tight and nervous whenever he does.

"I am just a born pessimist," she frets to herself, waiting for Martin to start.

He gets immediately down to business. "We seem to have some problems, Maryanne. Generally, things are going smoothly. The snag seems to be with some of the typing and some of the filing along with the billing. What do you think you can do to clean things up a little?"

Maryanne sighs but does not respond.

"What do you think? Is there any hope for it, Maryanne?" Martin asks, trying to relax the discussion.

Finally, the office manager says, "I'm worn out from trying. It is exhausting, trying everything there is to try and people are still not satisfied. I will try to straighten it out, but don't have much hope."

Martin leans toward Maryanne and says, "Maryanne, you have been with me from the beginning. To tell you the truth, I'm beginning to get some heat about you, about your performance. There is some question about whether you can handle things anymore with the computers and all. I don't know. I think you can do it, but you need to tell me what has to happen to get things straightened up."

Maryanne sits motionless, not saying anything until Martin settles back to outwait her. In a small voice, she reluctantly says, "You'll have to decide for yourself about me. I am working as hard as I can. I've given this firm all I have. Things are a mess around here. I'm a nervous wreck from trying to straighten out everything that goes wrong. Everyone thinks it's all my fault. I suppose they are right. I'm just one person and can't do it all. It must all be my fault. Even you think it is all me, now."

Martin can feel his ambivalence. Part of him wants to hang tough with the office manager and the part that has known Maryanne for years wants to straighten things out for her. As he tries to get control of his feelings, Maryanne says, "It's no wonder I get so nervous and upset. Things keep changing. About the time I get one thing straightened out, it's something else. It's like riding a roller coaster. It is more than anyone can be expected to handle. I guess someone needs to be the scapegoat, though."

Martin does not know what to say now. Maryanne has been with the firm too long just to fire. Anyway, that is not his style. When good people are not getting the job done, pointing the finger at them is not the way to go.

"People around here care about you and want things to be comfortable for you, Maryanne."

Maryanne looks down at her hands as she says, "I need this job, but it's not my life. I work because I need to work, but it's not the center of my life. The things and people who are important to me are not at this office. When I'm here— which is a lot more than I am getting paid for—I give it 100 percent. I think my seventeen years prove that. I don't know what you're going to do about the problem you have. It's for sure I can't work any harder."

The conversation does not end so much as it dies. Maryanne leaves without saying anything more. Martin is at a complete loss. He takes a deep breath, rubs his chin, reaches for his phone and asks his secretary about his next appointment.

DISCUSSION

Maryanne plays bummed out to perfection. Her main strategy is to get Martin—her protector—to feel sorry for her.

- "I am worn out from trying"

- "It is exhausting, trying everything there is to try and people are still not satisfied"

- "I have given this firm all I have"

- "I am just one person"

- "Even you think it is all me, now"

- "I guess someone needs to be the scapegoat"

Let Martin get tough with Maryanne and then give him a guilt check. On a scale from one to ten, he will register at least eight or nine. Maryanne is counting on it.

As an aside, you occasionally see an interesting variation on the theme. The bummed out player makes an alliance with several other players. As a bummed out diad or triad, the crew supports each other's bummed out patterns. People who play together survive together. They usually describe their shared condition as being burned out or perhaps demoralized.

Maryanne takes full advantage of Martin's compassion. It enables her to use several more bummed out techniques most creatively.

"I will try to straighten it out but do not have much hope," is integrated smoothly into her play. Maryanne does not expect to succeed and goes on to make it clear that it is not her problem anyway.

"I don't know what you are going to do about the problem you have."

She sets up an airtight and criticism-proof place to hide. She tells Martin that she cannot fix the problem and makes sure he understands that it is his problem and not hers. She gets points if things get better and loses nothing if they stay the same or get worse. At this rate, she is good for at least another seventeen years.

The next technique Maryanne uses is central to playing bummed out. It is hard to spot, though. No matter what happens, the player must not defend or stick up for himself.

Martin says, " . . . but to tell you the truth, I am beginning to get some heat about you, your performance." Notice that Maryanne never responds to this or to any other implication that she might be inadequate or at fault.

"I am just one person and can't do it all. It must all be my fault." Anyone who hears any acceptance of responsibility or culpability in this is a prime candidate to become some player's protector. Even a beginning counter player can hear the real messages.

• Get off my back

• Quit kicking me when I am giving it everything I have

• I can take it from them so long as you are here to protect me

Being negative about almost everything is essential. Being nervous and uptight is a good touch too, a sign of an experienced bummed out player. Look at Maryanne's behavior and posturing as she waits for Martin to start the meeting. Along with being tense, she reminds herself to be negative: a pessimist, as she calls it.

Maryanne wants no part of anything positive. Martin says, "Generally, things are going smoothly." Not only does she fail to respond to this, Maryanne reminds Martin from time to time that it is a negative environment.

- "Things are a mess around here"

- "It is like riding a roller coaster"

- "It is more than anyone can handle"

Maryanne also remembers to remind Martin about her nervous condition. "I am a nervous wreck from trying to straighten out everything that goes wrong." For good measure, she brings it up again. "It's no wonder I get so nervous and upset."

Maryanne does not devalue herself, although this does work well for bummed out players in a pinch. She plays the next best card, though. She devalues everyone and everything else.

"The things and people who are important to me are not at this office."

The things and people who are important to her are somewhere else. Yes, that is exactly what she says. Martin is not important to her. Her job is not important to her. The people she works with are not important to her. Neither the law firm nor its clients are important to her.

Listen well Martin Koch. Maryanne is telling you something important. It may just have something to do with why there are problems in her area.

What do you think, Martin? You do not think, do you? You go with your feelings instead of going with what Maryanne is telling you. Keep it up. Maryanne is counting on it.

Successful bummed out players are experts at spotting and using people like Martin; and these players are in no danger of extinction. There is usually a Martin for each Maryanne.

IN BRIEF

Bummed Out players do not expect to succeed

When bummed out is the game, the player neither values nor expects job success. Should it come, it is only serendipity. His personal priority is being protected and being forgiven—in advance—if things go badly. It is this guarantee of immunity that the player works for.

Skilled bummed out players never make commitments by saying things like:

- "I'll take care of it"

- "Consider it done"

- "You can count on me"

Instead, they say:

- "I'll try"

- "I'll give it my best shot"

- "I'll make a run at it"

- "Let's hold our breath and hope for the best"

Bummed Out players do not stick up for themselves

This may be the trickiest part of playing bummed out. There is a natural temptation for the player to lash back, defend himself, and react to attacks, especially on his ability, credibility, or integrity.

Say to the player, "You are not trying. You are not giving me your best. You are in over your head. I can't count on you." No matter how tempted the player is to defend himself or aggressively react, these impulses are absorbed and not responded to in any way. He hangs his head, tucks tail, and takes it. The trick is for the player never to forget that he is bummed out.

If his assailant does not back off, the bummed out player needs to find his protector to deal with the attacker. If worse comes to worse and he cannot get himself rescued, he passively sits there and takes it.

Bummed Out players are negative about everything

Being bummed out and being negative are two sides of the same coin. As with other versions of The Frustration Factor, negativism is a frequent feature. For the bummed out set, though, being negative is the main effect. Remember, the effect is all there is to being bummed out. The key is that the effect is not always present for the player. That is what separates being bummed out from being depressed.

Depression is a psychological disorder. It underlies difficulties like eating and sleeping problems, a generally flat or unexpressive mood, and unpredictability in attitude or behavior. The main feature is often a change in the person's normal pattern of behavior and adjustment. Like Maryanne in the illustration, being bummed out is a way of life at work. What would be learned if anyone bothered to check is that there are times away from work when she is not that way at all. In fact, she is probably not bummed out at work all the time. It mostly comes up when things get tough, when there are problems, or when she is about to become the focus of criticism. The truly skilled player can turn being bummed out on and off at will, timing it to match the situation. The trick of the expert player is never to get too far away from the bummed out affect. When it is show time, the performance cannot seem forced or faked.

Bummed Out players are uptight or nervous

With the bummed out player, being uptight and nervous appears natural and never seems put on. The player usually points out the condition. "I am a nervous wreck." Also, his posture is either stiff or somewhat slouched. The impression is of someone who is hyperalert and on guard or someone who has surrendered to the inevitable. Small closed gestures are also a must. Hands folded on the lap add to the effect as does an occasional hand to the mouth. The notion is to give the impression of having been through the wringer.

The most effective tool of the bummed out player is the voice, though. Players learn to talk in a little or quiet voice. Swallowing while talking helps the effect, if the technique is not too obvious. It is also important to talk slowly, as if talking at all is a real burden. The aim is to give the impression of a whipped puppy. The player, however, needs to be sure not to overdo it.

*Bummed Out players do not deal well with the ups
and downs of organizational life*

In the illustration, Maryanne refers to the law firm as a "roller coaster." Amusement parks are a real turn on for many people; but for bummed out players, the environment is far from amusing. As a technique, "ups-and-downs phobia" is up there with the best.

The game works like this. When things are in a turmoil and not going smoothly, the player says, "Things are always a mess around here. Just about the time I get a handle on one piece, either it changes or something else goes to pot."

Alternatively, if things are stable and running like clockwork, the player says, "Nothing ever changes around here. No one wants to deal with the problems. It is either just sweep them under the rug or ignore them and hope they will go away."

There is also a little twist at the end if the player is exceptionally skilled. He says, "Sometimes I feel like I'm the only one around here who gives a tinker's damn about this place." Expert bummed out players know it is the little things that get the job done.

*Bummed Out players do not value the people
and activities in the organization*

This is a necessary part of being bummed out. It is expressed in a variety of ways but usually needs to be verbalized to be effective.

- I am beyond caring

- I wish everyone would leave me alone and let me just do my job

- I do what I am paid to do. The rest of that stuff is not my concern

- When it comes to this place, I can take it or leave it and would just as soon leave it

It is important for the player to be careful, though. The lines have to be delivered in a way that seems to convey the opposite message. "I am beyond caring," needs to be delivered in a way that conveys, "I care so much and so deeply that caring is causing me pain." The notion is that whatever the problem is, it is breaking the player's heart.

Bummed Out players do not have much energy

This is also a must for the bummed out player. The need is to create the illusion of low energy while behaving the opposite. It is a martyr kind of thing. No matter how exhausted the player is, he needs to be the first at work and the last to leave. Working through breaks and over lunch helps the cause. The player needs to be sure to take breaks and lunch at irregular times. It will not do to get actually exhausted. Being a bummed out player requires being rested and in top form, for he is sacrificing all for the organization.

MANAGEMENT TIPS

Going at it with a skilled bummed out player is exhausting but is not particularly difficult. Be careful that bummed out is a regular pattern of play for the specific player. Watch that it is not an indication of depression in a colleague who is normally not that way. The key is to see that the authentic bummed out player goes into the routine mostly when he receives criticism or when there are problems. If you are looking for it, the pattern is easy to spot.

Consider first what the dynamics of the play are. The bummed out player is using the technique to avoid responsibility, to get others to back off, and to avoid work or pressure. In a child, the pattern would be called pouting.

Once you spot the bummed out player and understand his behavior, the next step is to locate his protector. No, it will do no good to confront the protector. He either will not hear you or will in some other way refuse to do anything about the problem.

When the player plays or the protector protects, it is time for counter play. It also will do little good to talk with the bummed out player about his behavior, but it cannot hurt. At least talking about the problem helps put the player on notice that he will not be successful playing the game with you. Whether you talk to the player or not, there are two actions that are necessary and almost always effective over time.

First, simply outwait him. Bring up a problem or issue of concern and then wait for a response other than the bummed out kinds of things discussed above. If necessary, say, "I hear all that. My concern is . . . I'm waiting for your response to the problem." Patiently go back again and again until an appropriate response comes. If necessary, say, "I can see you are not going to deal with this, and I do not have time to play your game. Have your response to me in writing in two hours."

The idea is first to respond only to positive and productive behavior. Next, set things up so such behavior is expected and required. At first, the player will likely not follow through or do what you expect. When this happens, it is time to say, "I expected you would handle this. It seems to me you are either unwilling or unable to deal with these kinds of things. Since it is important, I'm going to take some other action to be sure it gets done. It's too bad you are unable to handle your job. We will need to talk about that soon." Do what needs to be done to get the job done. Interestingly, the bummed out player is likely to do the job himself the next time.

You will be well-advised to think about where these confrontations take place. The bummed out player has a tendency to sit and not talk or respond. If this happens in your office, it may be difficult to stop the process, to get the player out of your office, and get onto other things. If the interaction or lack of interaction is somewhere else, you can be the one to leave. This makes it more convenient and keeps the player from having control of your space.

Sooner or later—and probably sooner—you will need to deal with the player's protector. He will come to the aid and defense of the player. Especially, if the protector is your organizational equal or superior, it is not a good idea to confront him about his protector role.

If the protector confronts you about your approach with the player, say, "I am not sure what you are talking about. Andy (the player) seems to be having a rough time of it. My problem is getting the job done. All I did was to make arrangements to be sure the job gets done. Andy needs to work out his problems, but we need to take care of business in the meantime. If Andy can do the job, that will be terrific. If not, the job still has to be done. Why don't you talk to him about that? Maybe you can help him work out whatever the problem is. You seem to have a special relationship with him. I just need to be sure the work gets done, one way or the other." Even the most committed protector is likely to understand and accept this kind of reasoning. If not, he is likely another experienced player who needs to be managed separately from the original player.

Chapter Five

Committee Players

Committee players are not so much a type of player as they are a collection of players sharing traits and behavior. Within the group, there are subgroups that have their unique methods and techniques. It is a committee kind of thing. In the illustration, you can see the various types of committee players. It is hard to put these players into a situation that highlights their play and also draws attention to their dysfunctional behavior. To be sure you can see how these players drive you and everyone else up the wall, I created a silly situation that is almost as outrageous as the play. Not doing this runs the risk of representing committee play as a normal and reasonable part of day-to-day organizational life. It is normal but somewhat less than reasonable. The illustration is thus a cartoon-like event that emphasizes the play or the lack of play, depending on your perspective. You can mentally move the exaggerated behavior into your organization and compare it to your experience. I think some of the players will be familiar to you.

ILLUSTRATION

The Frustration Factor Society International (FFSI) advances the art and science of driving people up the wall throughout the world. The committee on methods is meeting in Chicago a week late. They were to meet in San Francisco, but the location subcommittee neglected to reserve a hotel. Only a few of the sixty-three members are present because of a little snag with the meeting notices. Even with this glitch, the committee is now meeting.

Mark Brown, a charter member, is trying to make a motion to raise "Not Me" to a recognized method. "It may be that we might want possibly to consider Not Me as a method."

Another member asks, "Are you making that as a motion?"

Mark says, "Well, not exactly. Maybe we can talk about it and see what everyone thinks."

Steve clears his throat and starts the discussion. "It's the kind of thing where it is easy to see both sides." Steve squirms a little in his chair. Seeing that no one else wants to talk, he says, "I could come down on either side of this one. If Mark is solid with this one, I am not saying I could not be persuaded."

Sharon Lewis, from Texas, hesitatingly joins into the discussion. She says, "I thought, well, I have been at a few meetings where the person who brings up an idea makes the motion. I would like to suggest Mark puts his idea in the form of a motion."

Mark nervously jumps in. "Oh, no. I don't think I should be the one to head this up. It should be someone with more experience or specific interest. James, from Kentucky, always knows the right words for things like this."

The committee silently fumbles for a few minutes, waiting on James to take the lead until Mark notices that James is not there. In response to his discovery, Mark says, "James does not seem to be here. We could put this off until he is able to attend a committee meeting."

Sharon says, "I'm not sure we should do that. Maybe we should, but we don't want to be too quick to box ourselves in. Waiting on James is only one of our choices."

Brad, from Philadelphia, thoughtfully enters the debate. "Sharon may have a good point. I want to hear some ideas from the rest of you before coming to closure on this one. Whenever we decide to break, it might be well to chew on this one a little over lunch."

Sharon is quick to agree. "I'm going to hang with Brad on this one, unless someone has a better idea."

Tim, from Maine, feels like it is a moment tailor-made for an apple polisher like him to say a few words. "I believe in consensus and think we can all agree on one thing. The members who are here today have struggled with this important decision. We have to tread lightly in sensitive areas like this. It's people we are talking about here. The extent to which any decision might offend someone has to be considered each time. Sure, there is the other school of thought that encourages quick decisions and an ability to give varying priorities to the elements of the process. Nonetheless, getting members unnecessarily upset is not the way to go either. I think we have come to the right decision based on what we know right now."

Wanda, from Washington, is observing the discussion intensely and chooses this point to join in. "I think this might be a good time to bring up the consideration of another method for recognition by our committee. I'm talking about the apple polishers. I don't think it's appropriate to mention names, but just maybe there is one among us who has mastered the method well enough to talk about it." She then looks at Tim from Maine.

"Who, me? No, not me. I'm not the one to speak on this one. You should go ahead, Wanda. You are so much better than I am at that sort of thing."

Smiling her perpetual smile, Wanda says, "Let's not get into a hassle about this. It is not important enough. Working cooperatively together is the key to success. Who speaks is not worth the stress. I will withdraw my suggestion in the interest of harmony."

It takes a half hour or so of small talk to clear the air and give everyone a chance to mellow out. Jami, from Oklahoma, tentatively brings the group's attention back to the task at hand. "I have been thinking about the issues we have before us. I wonder if it might be a good idea to call a few of the members who are not here to get their thoughts on things."

Jami's idea stimulates instant, positive expressions and the project is under way. Because no one has a committee membership list, Jami makes a list of the members the committee can remember. The committee manages to divide the list; and as Jami gives Ted, from Ohio, his names to call, Ted says, "Not me. I would like to help, but I have some stuff here I had to bring along to work on. I can't step away from it. Either I'm going to whip it, or it's going to kill me first. The pressure is too much sometimes. You know how it goes."

It is a little after 12:30 when the members start getting hungry enough to say anything. To this point, no one wanted to break the flow of the meeting or be the one to bring up lunch. It might be seen as a lack of interest. The need for food and the call of nature finally gets the best of Wanda, though.

"I am going to excuse myself. I must have had too much coffee."

Rather quickly for the committee, the members support Wanda's decision. Let it suffice to say that looking in on the afternoon session that starts an hour and a half late is redundant.

DISCUSSION

As I mentioned earlier, the committee meeting is more of an animated cartoon than a serious deliberation. The problem is this. Any meeting and the behavior of the participants take on importance in proportion to the purpose of the meeting and the topics discussed. The perceived status of the participants is also an element. If important people are meeting to discuss important things, the meeting is important. For you, this conditioned perception has to stop. There are ample opportunities for players to drive you up the wall at any meeting from trivial to critical, from mundane to the summit.

Looking at the FFSI committee meeting is instructive. While doing this, it helps to supplement that examination with parallels to what may be more familiar situations. This is in no way intended to diminish the importance of the committee meeting.

Committee players who are into "Not Me" have to stay away from positions of responsibility or circumstances where they might be expected to have a strong opinion. Their game plan calls for tagging onto the plans and decisions of others and riding them to power and influence. They are very good coattail riders.

"It may be that we might want possibly to consider," is a classic in the archives of behavior that can drive you up the wall. The attempt is to introduce "Not Me" as a recognized method. Mark Brown not only manages to introduce the idea, he gave the members an example of the method. If anyone objects, Mark can simply say, "As you could tell, I was a little uncomfortable bringing it up. I told someone back home I would at least raise the idea. I told him I was not sure it would fly."

Suppose another committee member says, "I like the idea. Some of my best friends are what you might call the "Not Me" type."

Mark can then say, "It may be worth considering after all. I know a "Not Me" type or so myself." If a third member says, "I think the idea stinks." Mark can then say,

"I see the two of you have some thoughts about this. I will appreciate the opportunity to listen to your discussion."

At that point, Mark sits back to listen, waffling back and forth a little, depending on who seems to be winning the debate. If one debater comes away a clear winner, Mark joins the victor. He tries to placate the loser with, "I would like to go along with you on this one. I am a little inclined away from your position. We'll get together on the next one, though."

Instead of the committee in the illustration, suppose Mark Brown is in a sales meeting at the insurance agency where he works. Dean Tylor approaches Mark for support for a plan to pitch a new policy to a company in town. Dean presses for support and gets what he thinks is Mark's commitment. At the sales meeting, the boss leans a little away from Dean and toward another salesman. The moment of truth has arrived.

Dean asks, "What do you think, Mark? We would all value your thoughts, especially given your experience in the community."

Sorry Dean, kiss that deal goodbye. Never think a player like Mark does not know which side of the fence to sit on.

Mark takes a long, thoughtful breath and says, "I could come down on either side of this one. I am not saying I couldn't be persuaded."

Steve from the illustration is not a piker in the "Not Me" department either. Notice how he and Mark from the above insurance example could be twins. In the illustration, Steve says, " . . . it is easy to see both sides. . . . I am not saying I could not be persuaded." Along with some question about what it is he is not saying, what he is saying is similarly unclear. The key to Steve's success as a player is that he does not say anything. He leaves things open for any decision, including no decision. He can wait until a decision comes along and then use that one, acting as if it were his position all along. In the meantime, he appears to be an active participant in the decision process.

Put Steve in a different context. The City Commission is meeting. Steve is the chairman. A member of the audience joins the Commission's discussion in violation of the rules. Steve tries to get the intruder to stay out of the discussion.

The speaker says, "What kind of town is this where a common citizen cannot talk? Are you telling me I cannot have a say in the government of my city?"

It is easy to imagine Steve's saying, "I would never say anything like that. It is only that there may be a better place and time for this. It is still important that the Commission hears the views of everyone who wants to talk. I am only saying there is a time and place for things like this. There is a lot on our agenda tonight. It is always important to keep an open mind, though. I want you to know I'm ready to talk with anyone, anywhere, at any time. I hope this clarifies things for us here tonight."

The odds are about 80/20 that the intruder sits down and stays quiet. Most people are polite. Steve is counting on it. If the citizen gets pushy, Steve is counting on another member of the Commission—any other member—to help him deal with the problem. He lets someone else argue with the common citizen. Steve says, "Just Not Me."

In the illustration, Sharon shows the fuzzy boundary between "Not Me" players and the apple polishers. "I'm going to hang with Brad on this one, unless someone has a better idea." In one short sentence, she manages to cozy up to Brad. She disclaims any responsibility for the idea. Additionally, she puts everyone on notice that she will jump ship if a better or safer opportunity comes along. Sharon is in a great position to polish the first apple presenting itself to her. For the true aficionado, Sharon uses a very strong mix of techniques.

Put Sharon in a different setting, and the full power of her play comes to the forefront. Keep in mind the extra touch. Sharon is chronically cheerful and usually downright perky. She shows enthusiasm in endless supply for almost anything and virtually never gets upset unless it is to her advantage. She is a very skilled committee player.

Sharon is at the final meeting of the selection committee where the new chairman of the English Department will be chosen. There are three finalists for the position. Each has two supporters on the seven member committee. Sharon is in the position to cast the determining vote: not an enviable place for a committee player.

Sharon has the full attention of the other six members. They are waiting for her to vote. With a smile and even more energy in her voice, she says, "This is super! This is what the process is all about, isn't it? What we have here are three fine candidates, any one of whom will serve this great institution admirably. It is a banner day for us. The important thing is for us to all be happy with the decision we make. Being happy with our choice is the most important part of what we are all about. What I am going to do right here and now is set aside any selfish interests or motivations. I make this commitment to each of you. I commit myself to staying here as long as it takes for us to make a choice that is comfortable for all. Can *we* do this? Can we each commit to hang in there for the good of our school and for our students?"

If a committee member says, "Get off it, Sharon. It's your turn to vote, so vote." Sharon takes on a shocked and hurt expression and says, "You disappoint me. I cannot believe you want to sacrifice the department and our students just to save a little time by rushing a decision as important as this."

It makes no difference what happens next. Sharon has moved the issue at hand away from selecting a new chairman to matters of school spirit and loyalty. It reduces to who cares the most and Sharon wins hands down.

The players in the illustration modeled an additional method worth noting. Along with the Not Me players and apple polishers, the committee on methods gives a glimpse at some "poor me" techniques. The key to "poor me" success comes through getting others to feel sorry for or excuse the player. Let it suffice to highlight an example from the committee.

"Not me, I would like to help; but I have some stuff here I had to bring along to work on. . . . You know how it goes." The socially correct response is, "Sure, I know how it goes." Ted, from Ohio, is counting on people giving him this response. The result is that the committee excuses him from helping.

Suppose some social incompetent says, "I don't know how it goes at all. It just looks like you're trying to get out of helping. You are no busier than the rest of us." Speaking up probably feels good but does not work. Ted simply says, "Good for you. It's nice everyone doesn't have to go through this. I hope you keep your charmed life. A dog should not have to work this hard. Maybe I will have a small reprieve and have time the next time you need some help. I always like to pitch in when I can."

Ted's maneuver speaks for itself.

IN BRIEF

Committee players never take the lead

- He who hesitates is lost

- Strike while the iron is hot

- Victory belongs to the swift

These statements represent the thoughts of a moron from the committee player's point of view. Any second-rate player knows that the truth lies in a different set of wise sayings.

- Follow the leader

- There is safety in numbers

- Fools go where angels fear to tread

- Look before you leap

- Do not overrun your blockers

- Let the other guy show his hand first

- The early worm gets caught by the bird

Yes, this sounds more like philosophy for the committed committee player.

Committee players are wishy-washy

Do not confuse this with going whichever way the wind blows. The trick is that a good player does not go at all. The master just stays in one place and leans with the wind or the crowd. The direction totally depends on the situation or who the player is talking with. The game is potentially dangerous, however. The player must not go far enough in any direction to expose himself to a charge of changing horses in the middle of the stream.

A player is talking to Norma. "There is a lot of truth in what you are saying. It's easy enough to see where you're coming from. I think you should stick to your guns."

An hour later, he is talking with Glenna, the person with whom Norma was having the problem. "It is a real problem, Glenna. It looks like the hassle would get to you after a while. I'm just glad it's not me who has to deal with that one."

The next day, the committee player is talking to Norma and Glenna together. "As I have shared with both of you, things around here are a mess sometimes. It's a sad thing when dedicated people like the two of you are at each other."

This player is truly a person for all occasions.

Committee players cannot make decisions

The point of primary interest here is that skilled players appear to make decisions when there is no decision.

A subordinate asks, "What should I do about this?"

The player says, "Use your best judgment."

The problem is that the subordinate's best judgment was to ask the boss.

In another example, a colleague asks, "How would you go with this if you were me?"

The player says, "That is a tough one. I think if I were you—and I am sure glad I'm not—I'd check with some other people to see how they handle that kind of thing."

Of course, asking someone else is exactly what the person is doing when he asks the committee player.

In another situation, the player is asked, "What have you decided? It is past time to do something."

He says, "At this point it is a no-win kind of thing. Let's just wait and see what happens."

The player's strategy is to get the other person to make the decision, if there must be a decision. If it works out, the player takes credit for a successful mutual effort. If not, he shows endless compassion for the person who made the wrong choice. As a last resort, he holds his breath and hangs loose. Most of the time, things work out okay anyway.

When they do not, the player is simply a victim of unavoidable circumstances.

Committee players ride the coattails of others

This is a wait and see technique where timing is everything. The player waits to hear someone else express an opinion or make a decision and then steps toward the train. The critical timing is taking care to wait until the last minute to get onto the train. If the player commits too early, he can end up on the wrong train. If too late, he misses the train altogether.

It also helps to align with people in power. This, however, is a risky business. Power tends to be illusive and may not be there when expected. In big organizations, this is especially risky. The fun-and-games politics are such that fortunes can change overnight. Committee players are usually well-advised not to play in such unstable realms. Better they stick to watching the train and getting aboard only if it is moving out of the station. The track to the top that way is a little slower but much safer.

Committee players bend over backward to avoid offending anyone

In some settings, these players are good old boys or good old girls. In old movies, they are rich types—usually men—who do not work and hang around the club. The amazing thing is they almost never get upset about anything unless everyone else feels upset. Even then, you get the impression that they are upset mostly about others feeling upset.

For example, a small company is laying off twenty-five employees, including the committee player. He goes around sympathizing with those getting laid off, congratulating those who are staying, and telling the boss she has a rough job. In the meantime, he does no work and talks about how tough this is for everyone. No one gets upset with him because he is so pleasant and thoughtful. He is a good old boy. Of course, his play is to be seen as such a good old boy that the decision to lay him off will be withdrawn on that basis.

Committee players are too busy or stressed to pitch in

This is a double-edged example of The Frustration Factor. Not only does the player avoid extra duties or responsibilities, he gets others to feel sorry about how much pressure and stress he has. The payoff for this play is that people expect less than usual. It is like having your cake and eating it too.

Lewis is a therapist at a counseling center. The usual expectation is therapists spend five hours a day in face-to-face therapy with clients. Lewis is averaging less than four.

His supervisor says, "I want you to raise your productivity a little."

Lewis says, "That also concerns me. I would like to take on some more clients but just don't know how I can right now."

The supervisor asks, "Why? What is the problem?"—a big mistake.

Lewis leans back in his chair and explains, "It's an odd thing. The clients I have right now are especially difficult and time consuming. Along with that, I seem to have an unusual amount of paperwork right now. I'm taking it home just to keep my head above water. If that were not enough, one of my children has been ill and out of school for a few days."

By this point, the supervisor is feeling badly about bringing it up at all. Maybe he is expecting too much of the player. The way to spot a real pro with the technique is, after a while, he does almost nothing, and no one hassles him or complains.

Committee players always have excuses
for not getting the job done

The key to success with the technique for the committee player is always to use an external excuse. This includes circumstances or events outside his area and outside his control. Here is the real secret. The excuse also needs to be outside the expertise or control of anyone else who is around. Complex equipment—especially computers—is a natural.

"I would have gotten finished, but the computer would not cooperate."

Late deliveries are also good. "I would be done, but the part, report, instructions were not to me on time."

Things like car trouble, baby sitter problems, hot water tanks going out, someone's misfiling or not filing things, planes being late and the like are good too. The player only needs to be sure to keep a log to keep track of how long it has been between using each excuse. For example, some-one might remember he got a new hot water tank last month. That could be embarrassing.

Players need also to know about the Law of Flat Tires. It says that if you tell your boss today that you are late because you had a flat tire, tomorrow morning you will actually have a flat tire.

Committee players take everything personally

This technique is the essence of committee play. If the player is not skilled with personalizing everything, he is well-advised to consider specializing in another method.

Usually, pouting or withdrawing are good ways to show something has been taken personally. Some players get away with getting irate or indignant. Experienced players try both and see which works the best in specific situations or with specific people. Most aficionados find adopting one approach or the other most all the time works best.

With this technique, there is a beginner's and an advanced level of play. At the beginner's level, the player gets upset and personalizes things directly affecting him. At the advanced level, the player takes things personally that neither affect nor involve him.

The advanced player says, "I'm indignant about what's going on with Linda back in billing. It is not right that she is the only one back there who didn't get a new desk."

The manager says, "There were only five new desks. She will get a new one the next time we order equipment. Anyway, she is the newest person in the unit."

Undaunted, the player hangs tough. "How do you think she feels. It is no fun being a second-class citizen. Those ladies have as much right to respect as anyone else."

The manager says, "What does respect have to do with this? I thought we were talking about desks."

Too bad! This manager has been outmaneuvered by an expert committee player.

MANAGEMENT TIPS

This chapter focuses mostly on "Not Me" and "Poor Me" players. Counter play with these committee players comes first in understanding that the methods are two versions of the same game. The players' motivations are in their desire to get special concessions, preferential treatment, or exemption from most responsibilities. "Poor Me" players achieve this by getting others to feel sorry for them because they are weak or handicapped in some way. "Not Me" players also want people to feel sorry for them. They appeal to the compassion in others and to their natural inclination to be reasonable and supportive.

As is true when managing most people who drive you up the wall, the key to effective counter play is in your seeing through the game and understanding the motivations. You need to be sure it is a game and not a real problem or condition, however. This means you need to watch the player for a while and evaluate the legitimacy of his reasons, excuses, and general behavior.

Once your best judgment says that a game is on, the counter play is straightforward. If the player waits for someone else to take the lead or make a decision, say, "I will wait for you to take a position on this."

Now, wait and be sure what the committee player says is actually a position or decision. If he is just jumping on the train, say, "You are just jumping on the train. This was not your idea and as far as I can tell, you have added no ideas of your own. Get on the train if you must, but do not think that I am playing your game."

Rough treatment? Sure, but the player's game is no less objectionable. The point is not to buy into the player's behavior and to refuse to accept his excuses. Set the same standard for action and participation for him as is held for others. When the player does not come up to the standard, call him on it, making it clear the game will not work.

Does this mean you must be rude or abrasive? It may. But usually, it only means that you need to be assertive and honest. Typically it is enough to state what you think about the player and his behavior. This is exactly what he is counting on never happening. His game is dependent on it.

For "Poor Me" and "Not Me" brands of committee play, you normally only need to consistently call the player on his behavior. Insist that he participates in productive and contributing ways.

Counter play also needs to be pursued for the "apple polisher." It can be harder to call these committee players on their behavior. It may be tough for you to say, "I am tired of your apple-polishing." Nonetheless, that is the idea that needs to be expressed. Here is an example of how the point can be made with style.

Suppose Bill is the player and you are in a committee meeting with him. You say, "I sometimes wish I had Bill's ability to emphasize the positive in others." Polish the apple just a little yourself. "I wonder if we would not all do well to focus on the real and critical issues at hand though. I would like for us to consider . . . This seems to me to be where our efforts will be most productive."

As a skilled manager, you are careful but should counter the committee player on a continuing basis. The idea is to directly or indirectly point out the behavior and encourage discussion and action more related to the task at hand.

Chapter Six

Mainliners—
Havoc in the Organization

ILLUSTRATION

For over two years, the seventy-bed Rosewood Memorial Hospital, where Doug Blocher is the new interim administrator, has averaged a daily census of about twenty-five. The lack of patients has resulted in severe financial problems and serious questions about the quality of care.

By his second day on the job, Doug is ready to take charge. His first action is to cut the non-medical staff by one-third. Next, he orders the closing of the second floor. The patients and staff are to be crowded into the remaining space. He directs this done within sixty days. Finally, he orders a reorganization of the accounting department with no specific instructions other than to reorganize. Not bad for only two days on the job.

The third day, the Chief of Staff confronts Doug. "Don't you think you should have talked with me before sending out orders to disrupt everything?"

Doug looks surprised and says, "I didn't do anything to disrupt medical services. I only started some things to get the administrative operation running a little more efficiently."

The chief's exasperation shows as he says, "A hospital is a complex place. You can't start changing things without understanding how that will impact on other things. The people also have to be considered."

Doug is about to respond when the doctor is paged and quickly moves to other responsibilities. Doug also moves on.

There is a message on his desk to call the president of the hospital's board. Doug takes a deep breath as he listens.

"What are you doing over there, Doug?"

"I'm doing what you hired me to do. I'm getting this mess straightened out."

Doug taps a pencil on his desk as the president explains, "I did not expect you to go charging like a bull your first week. I thought you would take a few weeks to get familiar with the hospital and the problems, talk to people and you know, like that."

Doug is a little exasperated too as he says, "This is no time to change the expectations just because there is a little heat. I thought you wanted things straightened out."

It is Doug's lucky day. Just at that moment, the president gets another call and has to hang up. His last words are, "We'll need to talk about this when I have more time."

Things are working out well. Doug has more important things to do anyway. There is a job to do, and he is just the man to do it.

Ruth, Doug's administrative assistant, walks into his office. She is frustrated and annoyed about something. "You are going to have to do something about this one."

Doug raises a questioning eyebrow.

"Mrs. Markov is out here and she is irate again. Her husband owns the Rosewood Bank."

Doug smiles and says, "No problem. Send her in."

Mrs. Markov's problem is that she thinks the receptionist was rude to her. Without a second thought, Doug calls the employee and orders her to report to his office.

When she arrives, Doug says, "I will not tolerate the way you treated Mrs. Markov. I'm immediately suspending you for three days. I will not put up with that." The receptionist starts to respond but Doug waves her off and says, "I don't want to hear it. You heard what I said."

After the employee leaves, Mrs. Markov says, "I did not want anything like that to happen. You were too rough with her. I did not expect you to treat her worse than she treated me. It was not that big of a deal. I do not know what to say to you, but I expect my husband will want to hear about this."

Once he is alone in his office, Doug sits at his desk, trying to figure out what happened. In the middle of his musings, his phone rings. It is the personnel director.

"Doug, we have to talk. I am still dealing with the riot you started yesterday. Now I have a receptionist screaming in my face that you violated personnel policies. Give it another hour or so and we are going to have a complete walkout on our hands."

In a rushed tone, Doug says, "You'll need to follow up on this one for me. I don't have time for these kinds of details. I have more important things needing my attention right now. Take care of it and get back with me on the status of this issue. Give me a call if I can help."

The personnel director is momentarily speechless. By the time she gathers her thoughts, Doug has hung up and has moved on to other things.

On his way out of the administrative area, Ruth stops him with another problem. "It is the reporter from the *Times on* the phone. She wants a statement from you about the hospital's problems and your first week on the job."

Doug smiles and returns to his office where he talks to the reporter. "As the community knows, there are some serious problems. It is clear to me, though, the difficulties are all resolvable. I have started the process of improvement. There will be those who are unhappy and do not like the necessary solutions. It is strong medicine but the medicine has to fit the problems. I have things under control and expect things to be back to normal in a few days. Those who are unhappy need to understand that patient care is the first priority. We are on our way to a better future here at Rosewood Memorial."

Doug is barely off the phone when the president of the hospital walks into his office. "Doug, I am cutting to the chase with this. Let's get to the nub of it. We need to take a close look at how you are handling this and at what other options we have. People are up in arms."

Doug leans back in his large leather chair and says, "This is not one of those times where there are a lot of options. There are only two. We can back off and let the hospital go the rest of the way down the tube. Alternatively, we can follow through with what we have started. Those are the choices."

They talk back and forth for almost an hour. Doug finally says, "It may be time to bring in a systems analyst to look at the utilization problems. They interrelate with the serious personnel problems now surfacing. There are also issues in accounting and a major public relations problem. There are also the problems with the medical staff and their resistance to change. I could have some good people in here in a couple of days. We have a real crisis here."

The president quietly says, "I knew it was bad, but I did not know it was that bad. We better do something before it gets away from us. The town needs its hospital."

Once the president is out of his office, Doug takes a long breath and presses his fingers to the sides of his head. "That was a close one," he thinks. He wonders about what to do next. "I have to do something. The worst thing I could do now would be to back off. I would lose the respect of everyone. Just do something! Poke at it enough and something will happen. What in the world do they expect? They want a miracle. Maybe I'll call someone. They may know what they are doing."

The pot continues to boil at Rosewood Memorial. Incidents keep popping off in what Doug sees as random and unpredictable ways. He sees no pattern. Nothing is related to anything.

Doug is again talking to the president. "I'm not sure how they managed to keep all this covered up for so long. I would not have believed it could be such a mess."

The president says, "Staff members are calling me. They say you are making matters worse. Is that possible?"

Without any hesitation, Doug says, "I have not changed my approach. I am handling things the same way I did from the start. There is no way to go at this but head-on. We are just getting it out into the open. I think we may have to accept the reality the hospital may not survive the neglect of the past few years. Looking for other options for medical care may be our most responsible option. At least, we have to have an alternative in the wings. Let's face it. We are talking about bad management. We just need to be ready."

Two months later, Doug is once more meeting with the president. Doug says, "We can look until the cows come home at the separate parts of the problem and at how to fix the little pieces. We must keep our focus on the big picture. It's not just a combination of little things. It's a crisis about to blow up on us. The time is here to solve this once and for all. We are just lucky I got the SRC group to help us out of this."

As a last try, the president says, "This is going to put the hospital out of business. This does not even consider the $20,000,000 the community will lose in assets and increased costs. All that is bad enough. I shudder to think about the disruption in services and the cost to the families using the hospital. Is it worth it?"

In a most conciliatory tone, Doug says, "The reality is we have no choice. It is the price of trusting people. At least, that will never happen to us again."

DISCUSSION

Doug's success as a player is impressive. He demonstrates how experienced mainliners plunge in with no need for preparation or planning. "By his second day on the job, Doug is ready to take charge." He probably spent his first day finding out where his office was and how to use the telephones. By the second day, though, he is ready for major action. It is this take-charge approach that puts Doug into a class by himself. He orders a reorganization of the accounting department with no specific instructions other than to reorganize. This style of play is the essence of his game. The casual observer may think that the staff reductions and closing areas of the hospital are the main theme. No, those actions are too obvious. The sweeping changes raise the most outrage, but the little plays do in the hospital. The big actions take time and afford people many opportunities to react. The small ones go unnoticed within the bigger crisis but erode the organizational foundations. Even if the major changes slow or stop, the infrastructure, the heart of the hospital, is weakened and ineffective.

By the end of his second day, Doug has set the inevitable and inexorable process into motion. As astute observers put it, "It is a done deal."

For Doug, the process is primary. The outcome of the process is secondary. Look at the process in relationship to the president's expected outcomes.

"What are you doing over there, Doug?"

"I'm just doing what you hired me to do."

The president explains, "I did not expect you to go charging like a bull your first week."

"This is no time to change the expectations just because there is a little heat."

What are the president's expectations? They go like this.

"Doug, you are not doing what I expect."

Doug then says, "I understand that you want me to do the job."

The president says, "Yes, but take it a little easier."

Doug then says, "This is no time to tell me you don't want me to do the job."

With no definition of what the job is, Doug wins unless the president says he does not want the job done. Of course he is not going to say that.

An example of how Doug does the job is instructive. He is a man of action. Doug never lets the facts or the other side of the story distract or confuse him.

"You are going to have to do something about this one."

Without a second thought, Doug calls the receptionist into his office. "I am immediately suspending you for three days. . . . I do not want to hear it. You heard what I said."

Doug does not need to hear the story, understand the facts, or figure out why the problem came up. He just takes decisive action. One reason he gets away with this approach is the way he deals with any repercussions from his behavior.

"Doug, we have to talk."

"You'll need to follow up on this one for me. . . . I have more important things needing my attention right now."

That a boy, Doug! Leave the details to those who take care of that kind of stuff for you. Given time, the accumulation of such details will overwhelm everyone. It will become obvious that only drastic action will get the job done. And when it comes to drastic action, you know that Doug is the man for the job.

To be an effective mainliner, a player needs to stay above the details and away from day-to-day difficulties and issues. If inadvertently pulled in, an experienced player appoints a committee. Alternatively, he postpones action until he has consulted with superiors or experts. This gives him time to revise his game. In a pinch, he focuses on the details in agonizing detail. The best play, however, is at the level of generalization or sweeping action.

Doug's conversation with the reporter from the *Times* is a worthy guide to effective play.

"As the community knows, there are some serious problems. It is clear to me, though, the difficulties are all resolvable. . . . It is strong medicine but the medicine has to fit the problems. I have things under control and expect things to be back to normal in a few days."

Doug is a mainliner who one day will be working for the State Department or as press secretary for a prominent politician. Listen to Doug's sweeping acknowledgment of the obvious. "There are some serious problems." Of course, Doug gives no detail other than to say that they are all resolvable. How will he resolve the problems? He will do it with strong medicine, whatever that is.

Equally flatly, Doug asserts that he has everything under control. The trick is to act like a winner so Doug simply declares quick victory.

Here is the key to the play. How does he define victory? He says that victory is getting things back to normal. Listen to it! The president may think he is there to get things away from normal, at least away from what has been normal for the Rosewood Hospital. No, not for a quality player like Doug. It sounds like his goal is to get things back to where they were when he started. Perhaps the president should know this. Maybe Doug will tell him. What do you think?

Mainliners simply declare near-victory. It always lies just around the corner. Also, they must ensure that everyone stays on board. People need to know they are on the winning team, and the only way to victory is to stick with the mainliner.

The president says, "We need to take a close look at how you are handling this and at what other options we have."

The president is unsure. He is thinking about whether he is on the right team. Doug is ready, though.

"We can back off and let the hospital go the rest of the way down the tube. Alternatively, we can follow through with what we have started."

The use of we helps further the team idea. Also note the reduction to one option: Doug's option. Of course, letting the hospital go down the tube is not an option at all. The choices reduce to one choice. Doug's game is the only game in town.

The president does give Doug some pause for thought. This is the point at which Doug grasps the straw that is his salvation and puts him in The Frustration Factor history book.

"It may be time to bring in a systems analyst. . . . We have a real crisis here."

Without drawing a hard breath, Doug suggests that they get someone in who knows what he is doing. Calling the savior a systems analyst is the key. The president might otherwise think Doug should straighten things out himself. The skilled mainliner never stays in a position where anyone expects him actually to get the job done on his own. How easy is this for Doug? You only need to listen to the president.

"I knew it was bad, but I didn't know it was that bad."

It is just that easy! In one stroke of genius, Doug is forever off the hook. Now, no one expects him to succeed, least of all the president.

Does Doug know how close he came to losing control of the process? He surely does. It is so close that he has to stop and think for the first time since arriving at Rosewood Memorial. "I have to do something. . . . Just do something! Poke at it enough and something will happen."

The way out remains uppermost in Doug's mind. He continues to poke, knowing his worst mistake would be to let things settle down or for anything to be resolved. The existence of the crisis is the best smoke screen he has to cover up his lack of any idea about how to improve the predicament.

"I have not changed my approach. . . . I think we may have to accept the reality the hospital may not survive. . . ."

The way out is at hand; the hospital may not survive. The circle closes. Doug is there because the hospital is in trouble and may not survive. Doug says that nothing has changed. It is clear what he means by back to normal.

Once he locks onto the way out, Doug stays on task. "We have to keep our focus on the big picture. It is not just a combination of little things. It is a crisis about to blow up on us. . . . We are just lucky the SRC group is there to help us out of this."

Doug goes out in a flourish. He combines several techniques into a single complex play. He draws attention away from the separate parts of the problem and from any possibility of someone's trying to fix things one step at a time. He generalizes by calling his approach the big picture. The idea is that big people look at the big picture and little people work on the details. His appeal is to the part of human nature that wants to be a big person—a big shot, if you will.

Just to make sure the technique works, he repeats himself. He says that it is not just a combination of little things. So as not to seem repetitive, he next calls the big picture a crisis that is about to blow up. It is a little like yelling **Fire!** in a crowded theater. His hope is that everyone panics, with Doug standing there ready to point out the exit.

In Rosewood, as is true in most places or situations, everyone does panic and Doug is ready. He has the SRC Group in the wings to save the day. The result is that Doug is the hero. He has pointed the way out of a crisis about to blow.

From interim administrator to super hero in one quick and continuous flight to the top! Dare I say that Doug made the trip by way of the mainliner? (You may know of the law of conceptual inertia. It says that if you make any problem complex enough, you will not be able to do anything about it, ever.)

IN BRIEF

*Mainliners go into things in disorganized
and unprepared ways*

For these players, their approach is to dive in without any pretense of or need for preparation or organization. They rely on their instincts and agility. They are usually from the group who never bothered to do their homework in high school. Later, they wrote their college papers the night before they were due, without concerning themselves with trivia such as a trip to the library. In a pinch, they used someone else's notes or reading list. The solution is always at hand if the player is observant enough and clever enough to recognize it. If worse comes to worse, they can always ask for an extension, using any of the thousands of perfectly legitimate reasons available to them.

Mainliners start before understanding what is expected

This technique is axiomatic for mainliners. To find out what is expected is a waste of time. The player has no intention of doing anything other than what comes to hand. This is called "winging it."

Someone once said that if you do not know where you are going, you probably will not get there. The mainliner says that if he does not know where he is going, wherever he ends up is where he was headed. If played right, the people who count define it as the only place to be. Ultimately, no one likes admitting getting taken for a ride, especially to somewhere he did not want to go.

Mainliners solve problems before knowing
why the problems came up in the first place

It is like a doctor doing surgery for an undiagnosed condition. The doctor raises the knife and slices. Quickly, the patient has a visible condition, usually with a lot of blood thrown in just for good measure. Now it does not matter how it turns out. If the bleeding stops, the doctor is a hero. If not, the doctor made his best effort, but the patient was too far gone to be saved.

When a mainliner in your organization creates a predicament, he tries to find a scapegoat for the problems. People ask, "Why do we have this problem?" The mainliner likes to say something responsive. Whenever possible, skilled players blame the problem on someone outside the organization or on an employee who has left. At a minimum, they attribute it to someone who is out of favor or someone who cannot defend himself. Should an explanation actually be forthcoming, the player refers to it as a cover-up or an attempt to avoid responsibility. "Double talk" is also a good term to work in somewhere. Finding out real causes and explanations is not in the player's best interest. People might start looking for valid explanations for problems as a routine behavior. This lays the player open to who knows what.

In the rare event that the player's scapegoat simply says, "I fouled up," the player will be quick to call it a lie. Yes, this is strong medicine, but the medicine must be stronger than the condition. Mainliners go on to say, "He would not just admit it like that unless there was more to it.

I don't have time to get to the bottom of this right now; but take my word for it, there is more to this than meets the eye." Sure, the player relies on his wits. Having people openly admit to fouling up is right up there in the ranks of things to be avoided with finding out what actually causes specific problems.

Mainliners know that there is not a best way to do things or to think about things

An experienced player would say that this is not exactly correct. Mainliners never like to have anything so clearly stated.

The player says, "There is not a best way to do it or to think about it."

He is not suggesting that there is more than one way. He means that there is no way—no way to get the job done, no way to think about the problem. Listen to how the gambit works.

Ask the mainliner, "What are our options?" Even more to the point, "What is the best way to deal with this? How should we think about it?"

The mainliner waits a while to respond, takes a long breath and says in a most sincere and worried voice, "I sincerely wish this were that kind of problem. I would like to tell you there is a simple answer. I wish I had the magic for you again this time. This one defies logic and quiets the voice of experience. We are on new ground. We will need to bite the bullet this time. We will just have to plunge in and hope for the best. I will give it my 100 percent best shot for you, as I always do."

The player's rule is to use a short sentence for a little problem. "This is a puzzler, but I'll give it a shot." The bigger the problem, the more verbiage he uses. In either event, the ploy is the same. Avoid definition at all cost. The mainliner wants to wing it.

Mainliners do the job without knowing how to do it

You likely can elaborate on this technique without the benefit of any further comments. It fits into and is consistent with the overall pattern for mainliners. The essence of the technique is seeing that "knowing how" only limits and inhibits the range and flexibility of the player.

Of course from his perspective, the mainliner does know how to do the job. The difficulty for non-players is in understanding what "knowing how" refers to. The uninitiated think that "knowing how" means you have specific knowledge and skills related to the task or problem. They also think experience with the task is useful. The mainliner understands that, for him, these kinds of things are irrelevant. The only skills needed are those of the mainliner.

The main requirement is an ability and willingness to dive in and to keep poking. Things will happen that sooner or later make the task not doable, the problem unsolvable. At that point, the mainliner either abandons the task or calls in a specialist. He then takes full credit for saving the day.

Mainliners see everything as new or unique

The player using this technique gets the benefit of a quirk of nature. No matter how small the task or minor the problem, it likely has some element or quirk that distinguishes it from similar tasks or problems. The more complex the task or the more serious the problem, the more points of newness or uniqueness the player finds. Regardless of how nearly the current situation matches others, the mainliner focuses his attention and energy on these points of newness or uniqueness.

Liz is an engineer assigned to troubleshoot a lockup problem with a computer installation at a small retail business. For some reason, the main application and the operating system are not interfacing correctly. The result is that the system is locking up and the business is having trouble staying open.

Liz's first approach is to say that the people operating the system are causing the problem. When this does not hold up, she next attributes the difficulties to a hardware problem or bug in the operating system. Again, the explanation does not stick. Finally, she reverts to type as an experienced mainliner.

There are a few minor deviations from specifications in the way the business uses the system. One part of the application is one no other customers use.

"You are the only user who has tried to use this function. It's only an add-on to the main application. We did not expect it to be used on a daily basis. That is what your problem is."

"Well, it's important for us to use this function. How soon are you going to fix it so it doesn't keep locking up?"

Sure, Liz knows just what to say. "This problem is unique to your system. You will need to exercise your support agreements with the hardware and operating system vendors. They will need to straighten out your problems with their installations before we can help."

"We bought the system from your company. Aren't you going to stand behind your sales?"

Liz is again ready. "We will support you 100 percent. Just as soon as you get the other problems worked out, I will see that you have a specialist assigned to the problem." A specialist? Yes indeed. That is someone, anyone other than Liz. That's the way to pass the old buck!

Mainliners do not divide problems into manageable parts

Mainliners focus on the big picture, the broader issues, the wider implications. Anyone who tries to reduce things to understandable parts has a little mind and cannot see the forest for the trees. Such people have a limited perspective and are—in a politically correct company—thought of as conceptually challenged.

People who are analytic and systematic are the nemesis of the mainliner. These spoilsports want to divide the larger task or problem into small tasks or problems most anyone can understand and work through. The mainliner must not let this kind of reductionist problem solving get started if he is to succeed.

The spoilsport says, "Let's make a list of each activity that is necessary to get the job done. We can then put them into some logical order and split up the tasks. By the time we get to the end of the list, the job will be done."

The mainliner responds, "That may be a good approach down the road somewhere. We are a long way from being there right now. It's not that simple. At this point, the need is for some policy direction and meeting of the minds. We need to set up a committee to struggle with the real issues first."

Alternatively, the spoilsport says, "People are at each other's throats. Everyone wants to blame everyone. It looks like everyone is trying, but some little things are getting in the way. Let's sit everyone down and find out exactly what they need and what they expect. Through that process, they can get things out in the open and at least understand each other's problems."

The mainliner responds, "It has gone beyond simple discussion. It is going to take more drastic action than simply having people talk together and work out their problems. A committee meeting won't cut it this time. We need some decisive action from the top."

Mainliners either avoid or obsess over the details

This is a timing technique used most effectively with the other tools of the mainliner. By this time, the value of the player's avoiding the details should be obvious. The nuts and bolts of most tasks or problems are in the details. Understand and organize the details, and even the most sticky issues tend to succumb.

A favorite application of the technique is, "Have you read the documentation explaining the problem and how it needs to be handled?"

The mainliner says, "I do not have time for this non-sense. I am tired of the paper passing. I can see the problem is still there. It is time to take definitive action to deal with this once and for all."

Somewhat less often, the mainliner needs to come at it from the other direction. Someone says, "We need to take some broad action. There are only two or three pieces getting in the way. It is time to stop swatting flies and get rid of the garbage."

The mainliner says, "This is much too serious to act in haste. Your plan may have some merit, but I want to be sure we have considered all the possibilities. It is always better to be safe than sorry. Let's bring together all the documentation and review it with each of the people involved. Let's be careful with this one."

MANAGEMENT TIPS

Mainliners who practice their methods on the job are not only difficult but are also dangerous. They can and will put all or any part of your business out of business. Just keep in mind that their play is always for the store.

Understanding the mainliner's motivations is easy. He does not want to be found out. The mainliner does not know how to do the job needing to be done and would rather foul everything up than admit the truth. The player's goal is to bluff his way through, no matter what the cost.

With this in mind, counter play proceeds like this. Do not accept excuses and explanations that are not factual or do not have a ring of truth. If things are getting worse, if problems are getting out of hand, if business is going down the tube, the likelihood is that you have a mainliner at work.

The best counter play starts with a clear notion of what the goal or task is. It then extends to defining what progress is. Finally, counter play sets specific criteria for deciding if things are moving toward or away from the goal.

If there is no movement toward the goal or especially if there is movement away from it, it is time to hold the player accountable. Listen to the excuses and explanations and then hold him responsible.

Much of the time and especially in technical jobs or in complex situations, knowing whether the problems are the work of a mainliner or are unavoidable is difficult.

Much of the time, a single person gets into a position where only he appears to be qualified to judge his work. As in the hospital in the illustration, those to whom the mainliner reports are not able to judge. Those in the hospital who are knowledgeable are potentially part of the problem. The result is that the mainliner has no accountability to anyone who can knowledgeably and objectively judge his work. He has, for all intents and purposes, a free rein.

The issue with mainliners is that no one knows how to separate problems caused by the mainliner's behavior from situations that are going sour despite reasonable and skilled action. If you have an active problem, the only counter play is to develop a strategy to evaluate the project and the people objectively. The key here is to be sure the plan includes outside people who are experts in the problem area.

For you, the best counter play is to know that main-liners can and will do in your company while they drive you up the wall, given the opportunity. Since you may not detect them until it is too late, any important project should be mainliner-proofed in advance. Built into every important project should be an evaluation or monitoring process separate from and not linked to the project. This process needs to include people who are qualified to judge every aspect of the project. They also must have the proven ability to tell when circumstances are the problem and when the people in the project do not know what they are doing. Just be sure that the monitoring activity is not itself a haven for a mainliner of its own.

Chapter Seven

I-Players

ILLUSTRATION

Ray Vinham stands up to a light round of applause and delivers his campaign speech to the Westover Leadership Coalition. It is the evening he has waited for since the day he joined the civic group. From that first meeting, he had known that his being president was critical if the club were to get out of its rut. He revels in the knowledge that his day has finally come.

"Thank you for the opportunity to tell you about my qualifications as they relate to the important work of our organization. I have been in this club for six years and have seen examples of success and examples of failure. I have learned from that experience and now stand before you to ask for your support in applying my experience to the problems and challenges lying ahead.

"I have seen us flounder from reliance on recycled projects and repetition of the past. I pledge to you a new vision not shackled by the temptation to look back when we need to look ahead. My presidency will bring a new motivation, a new energy, a plan that moves us eagerly into the future.

"You have my word, my personal commitment that I will give 100 percent to the progress of our club. I will not stoop to the level of petty bickering and self-serving arguments, to the level of individual interests, and to the pressure of divisive factions. Your president will stand above the commonplace and ahead of those who would hold us back. I will be the leader of all our members.

"I make my personal pledge to each of you to tell all without holding back. I will bring every issue to you and pledge not to participate in the good-old-boy network. I will strive to be seen as your leader and not as just one of the boys.

"What should the goals of our fellowship be? I have struggled with the answer and am struck by its simplicity. I need only look at my goals, my interests, my aspirations. Ray Vinham is an example of, a personification of, the body of our shared ambitions, our collective will. This is not self-serving or arrogant. I know those who know me will see I only intend for our venture into tomorrow to center on those dreams we all share. I only want what we all have worked for over the years.

"I also pledge to you I will not stretch for your support by giving a false impression. Ray Vinham will be your president. This is an important job that cannot be honored by washing dishes, by knocking on doors, by trying to outdo the hard work of our valued members. Your president's place is at the leading edge of planning and assuring our success with the largest project, with the smallest detail.

"Let me close by sharing with you the heart of my campaign. I will work twenty-four hours a day, every day, to be the standard by which leadership may be judged. I will use my position of leadership as a vantage point from which to bring to each of you the best.

"I ask for your support, for your vote."

Once Ray finishes, it is time for Bud Smith to give his campaign speech. He stands up, stretches and slowly looks around the meeting room. Somewhat haltingly, he starts. "Ray, that was a fine speech. You are a qualified man."

Looking several members directly in the eye, Bud continues, "I can sure see why you would want to vote for Ray. It's a little monkey-see, monkey-do, but I think I would do a good job too. Whoever wins, I'm behind him and for whatever you feel is best for the club. All things considered, I still think I will vote for me." Bud is almost seated when he adds, "Oh by the way, I guess I will still wash dishes whatever you decide."

DISCUSSION

It is instructive to see an experienced "I-player" one-up a promising but less experienced player. Ray is a beginner and does not stand a chance when up against a master like Bud.

It is interesting to review the techniques Ray uses, even if he is somewhat awkward and amateurish. It also is instructive to see how Bud "puts the screws," so to speak, to Ray's campaign.

Not counting the times Ray uses "I," his promising qualifications as an I-player quickly surface. Those who are not students of the I-method may think that it is bad form to be so self-aggrandizing or chest puffing in a meeting with friends. To the contrary, there is no better place or better way for the I-player to be sure everyone knows just how good he is. As I-players say, "If you don't blow your own horn, no one else is going to blow it for you."

Ray does not make the wrong move so much as he is just outclassed. Consider how Bud uses the same techniques as Ray uses, turning them to his advantage. "It is a little monkey-see, monkey-do, but I think I would do a good job too. . . . All things considered, I still think I will vote for me." The master packs multiple techniques into a small package and delivers it squarely on target.

Bud hits the bull's eye with his little bomb. The trick is in, "I think I would do a good job too." He offers no reasons or explanations. It is a fact based solely on the word of Bud. His use of "I" is enough justification. Granted, Bud does reduce the importance of the thing to monkey business before making the assertion, but it still stands on the strength of his saying it. This is I-Play at its most effective.

Ray uses a similar technique. He considers no motivations or interests but his. He rings eloquent as he says, "I pledge to you a new vision . . . a new energy, a plan that moves us eagerly into the future." He takes complete control, offering only his vision, his motivation, his plan. Ray is on a roll! He establishes himself at the center of everything, and only what he thinks, feels, wants, and needs are important.

From his position at the center, Ray looks out on, or perhaps down on, everyone and everything. What is even more remarkable, he tells the members that he will continue to do so.

"Your president will stand above the commonplace and ahead of those who would hold us back."

He comes very close to saying that he is above the common man but does not quite go over the edge. Ray knows I-Play can be taken too far. It is all right to look out and maybe even down so long as he does not give the impression of looking down his nose.

Ray goes for the big close. "I also pledge to you I will not stretch for your support by giving a false impression. . . . I will use my position of leadership as a vantage point from which to bring to each of you the best."

Ray is an up-and-coming example of The Frustration Factor in action. It is a promise of things to come. Should the club members ever elect him president, they will get exactly what he promises.

Just to be sure Ray knows who the master is, Bud puts the icing on the cake. "Oh, by the way, I guess I will still wash dishes whatever you decide." This is just Bud's little way of letting Ray know that he overplayed his hand.

IN BRIEF

I-players overrate their skills and abilities

This technique is at the essence of the I-method. No matter how good the player is, he represents himself as somewhat more qualified. It is not necessary to represent himself as the best. This is where Ray in the illustration goes too far. The trick is for the player to overstate his skills and abilities only slightly. If he does it effectively, the claims will seldom be contested. If he calls himself "The Greatest," it is likely that someone, somewhere, sometime will test him. If this happens, it is put-up or shut-up time. The I-player does not want this type of confrontation.

In the illustration, you see how Bud simply makes himself the judge without claiming that he is the best judge. At that level, no one tests him.

Using I-Play and the overstatement technique are effective ways to move on to bigger and better things. Nick is a young associate in a large accounting firm. Through the normal course of events, he has obtained several small accounts and the busy work of the more senior associates. His peers complain about having to do the uninteresting work of the senior people, but Nick actively asks for such assignments.

Over time, he talks with the senior associates more and receives additional complex and interesting assignments. His approach is always to be into things just a little over his head.

When asked to do something beyond his ability, Nick seldom defers. He passes only if he thinks he cannot bluff his way along. He usually manages to hang in there until he learns how to do the assignment or gets someone else to tell him how.

Once in a while, things turn out badly. At those times, Nick comes up with ways to move the responsibility to other people or point to special circumstances. The net outcome is that Nick is rapidly moving up in the organization. The trick is that he is doing this while seldom knowing what he is doing. The moral from this I-player's point of view is clear. It is easier to be a good player than it is to be a competent accountant.

I-players are not concerned about the motivations or interests of others

To use this technique effectively, the player must pull off a nifty deception. The I-player needs to seem interested in people, their motivations, and their interests. If this does not happen, others see him as cold and uncaring. The message to people must be, "I care about you and only have your best interests at heart."

Here is the deception. The I-player only concerns himself with personal goals and interests. The game is to develop a level of trust and inattention that blinds other people from seeing what is happening. Within this blind spot, the player does his work.

An example is instructive. Mel Lewis wants to be on the committee that recommends contract renewals for faculty. His motivation here is interesting. He is also on the committee that reviews teaching assignments and schedules. His goal is to get a schedule permitting him to keep his outside consulting job. This is how he plays the I-game.

First, he spends a few months cultivating relationships with two or three members of the contracts committee. This gets him the desired appointment. Next, he spends a lot of time talking to Dave Ryner who is up for contract renewal.

"I know you are up for renewal and that, with the cuts and all, you are on the cut list. I like you and want to do everything I can to help you stay." There is no cut list but there will be some cuts.

Mel keeps his promise and votes for renewal of Dave's contract. It would have been renewed anyway. Dave is relieved and grateful. Now comes the payoff.

As Mel expected, Dave gets the schedule Mel wants. It is now time for Mel to close the deal. In a warm and sincere voice, Mel says to Dave, "I'm surprised and disappointed you took my schedule after all we have been through together. I guess you had your reasons. I just want you to know this won't affect our friendship, though. I'm glad you were able to stay, although I'm not so sure about me since I've lost that consulting job. You know how it is with a family. It takes a lot of money. That is not your problem, though."

The bind for Dave is real. Whichever way he goes, Mel wins. If Dave trades schedules, Mel keeps his consulting job. If Dave does not trade, he still owes Mel one. Having markers out there is almost as good as winning today. The successful I-player may lose one now and then but mostly he wins.

I-players are above it all

This ploy works best when combined with the two above techniques. First the I-player represents himself as somewhat exceptional in the ability and skill departments. This enables him to justify being separate from or above everyone else. Second, the player cares so much and is so concerned that he has to stay distanced. This is the best position for him to be maximally helpful. He is definitely above it all.

The trick is to avoid appearing too good to get involved or to participate. Others must not see the player as someone who will not get his hands dirty. The idea is to become somewhat of a father figure or mother figure, as the case may be.

Frank is a very skilled I-player who manages to stay above it all, most all the time. His approach is to talk little, appear to listen carefully, and to take detailed notes. He frequently says, "I'll get back to you on that one." This enables him to avoid getting into the middle of things or into a position where anyone tries to deal with him as an equal. Interestingly, this includes his organizational superiors. When he does get back with people—which is about half the time—he says, "I can, or can't help you with this one." Almost no matter what, he ends up with others seeing him as leaning down to do them a favor. Sure, it is just a little trick but most effective. Over time, the number of people who see themselves as owing him favors grows, even though he has done virtually nothing for any of them.

I-players do not look beyond simple self-interest

This is critical for I-players. The technique is a version of not being concerned about the interests of others but is important enough to receive separate attention. It is more than a general observation about the behavior of I-players. It is a mandate for I-players who are successful.

Beverly is a heavy equipment operator for a construction company. She is a first-class I-player, which accounts for much of her success in her chosen vocation. Vick is her oiler and is responsible for keeping her machine in good running condition.

One Thursday, Bev notices that Vick forgot to complete part of his task and wonders whether to do it for him or just let it slide.

Her impulse is to spend the five minutes it takes to do his job. She can let him know she did him a favor and then collect the marker some day. It also is tempting to let it slide, knowing that one time is not going to hurt anything. She can still let Vick know she knows, giving her the upper hand—at least a little.

What is her choice? The debate takes her about two seconds. Bev shuts down her machine and finds herself some shade. Within a few minutes, the whole job is shut down because of the importance of Bev's machine to the project.

Within a couple minutes, the superintendent walks over and asks, "What is this all about? Why are you shut down?"

Bev takes another swallow of coffee and says, "My oil light is on. Someone will have to check it."

The superintendent asks, "Didn't Vick take care of it?"

Bev says, "I have my hands full operating the machine. I will get someone to take care of it, though, if you want me to help you out."

The superintendent says, "Someone better take care of it! I sure don't have time for this . . ."

Matter-of-factly, Bev says, "You got it, boss."

Is the boss upset with Bev? He does not know who to be upset with. Is Vick upset with Bev? No, she did not point the finger at him.

The winner is Bev and there are no losers. No losers unless you see the company and its production schedule as losers. This possibility is not important to Bev or to Vick for that matter. The best part of the play for Bev and Vick is that, even if the superintendent talks to Vick about what happened, Vick can blame it on unexpected problems with the equipment. For this, he still owes Bev one.

It is a two for one trick. Bev has a marker from Vick and a favor due from the boss. As you see, Bev simply pursues her self-interest.

I-players use themselves as the standard for everything

- If the player is interested, what others say and do is interesting

- If he is frustrated, things are a mess

- If something affects the player, it is important, and if not, it is irrelevant

- If the I-player likes it, it is good, and if not, it is bad

- If the player is happy, things are going well, and if not, things are falling apart

- As the I-player goes, so goes everything and everyone

Machell is a manager of a small department in a medium size company. The secretarial support and data management for her staff are handled by a central support unit. Machell knows that about half of the support staff are new and there are serious problems with the company's computer system. There are recurring filing problems, data discrepancies, and unusual slowness with typing. These problems are frustrating to Machell and contribute to some problems for her staff.

On the other hand, her staff is working on some new activities and projects. This places some new paperwork and data demands on them. Within Machell's operation, there are some problems that contribute to the difficulties with the support unit.

Machell does not so much as give a passing thought to sitting down with the support manager and figuring out better ways of dealing with things. A skilled player like her does not consider such ridiculous time wasters.

What does she do? She promptly calls her superior and vents her outrage with the crisis in the support area. "You are going to have to do something about this crisis!"

"What would you suggest, Machell?"

"I don't have time to straighten out other people's problems. I don't know what you are going to do about your problem. All I know is my staff can't be expected to work under these conditions."

Right on, Machell! You play "I" to perfection. Define a small problem as a crisis, and then point your finger at someone else and suggest that it is going to bring things to a halt. The payoff is that no matter what problems Machell's staff have now, they are because of the crisis that is not her fault or responsibility. No matter what happens, Machell wins. That is exactly the position the I-player strives for at all times.

MANAGEMENT TIPS

I-players are a breed apart from other players. Most people who drive you up the wall find their motivations in underlying insecurity or a sense of inadequacy. For the I-player, a different kind of process is going on.

When the I-player overrates his skills and abilities, you are not seeing an overcompensation or intentional exaggeration. The player truly believes his skills and abilities are better than they are. People say things about these players like, "If he were half as good as he thinks he is, it would be a thing to behold." The point is that the player may be competent at something or may be just average. Nonetheless, he perceives himself as being better than he actually is. Usually, this overrating of his ability is to the extent that the player honestly believes he is the best at whatever it is.

The player also believes that everyone else in your company is much less competent than he is at whatever it is. You can take it to the bank that everyone else includes you. The I-player is a superior person, he thinks.

This feeling of superiority reaches beyond skills and abilities. The I-player believes his issues are all that matter. The problems and interests of others are unimportant in comparison. The player acts as if he is above it all, and from his point of view it is true. The player's self-interest is of primary importance, and there is no reason to look beyond that.

The I-player indeed does believe he is superior. It is important never to forget this simple fact. Now consider the equally valid fact that the belief is irrational. The player is not the best at everything and especially not the best at getting along and working with others. Since the belief is irrational, talking with or confronting him about it will do little good. It will tend to reinforce the belief, as irrational as that might be.

What does effective counter play look like with the I-player? The key is not to buy into the game. Over time, most people will, for whatever reason, gradually come to treat the player as if he is better than anyone else. It may be just too exhausting or tedious to do anything else. The I-player is not called on his behavior. He gets privileges other people do not have. People listen to the player when no one is interested in what he is saying. People develop a tolerance for the I-player, are deferential because it is easier, and let the player have his way.

What to do? First, treat the I-player the same as everyone else. Do not give him special privileges. Do not listen unless what he is saying is of interest. Do not defer to him unless he is right. If you are to play successfully with the I-player, you need to be self-assured, assertive, and persistent.

For most I-players, being fair, firm, and consistent will be enough to affect change in their behavior. For the committed few, however, an additional technique is needed.

I-players do have problems, make mistakes, and get into difficult situations. Their approach is primarily to displace responsibility onto other people. It is not their fault; and they go to some length to be sure you know that. Here is what to do when you know you are dealing with an I-player.

Say, "I can see that this is a serious problem. It may not be your fault; but you are in the best position to handle it. Given your skills and experience, you are the logical choice to get us out of this crisis. I am directing you to pull together a team including the key people and to get this one fixed. I am delegating the authority and responsibility to you. Please take care of it." It is likely that the problem will quickly become less critical and that the I-player will be less likely to play his game with you the next time he has a problem. Just be sure to keep an eye on the situation. In the unlikely event that there actually is a crisis needing your intervention, you want to remain in a position to do what needs to be done.

One further technique may be useful if the I-player does not assemble the team but gets everyone up in arms. Wait until the next time he comes to you with a crisis that is, of course, not his fault. Listen to hear who he is blaming this time. Suppose his target is Sue. Say, "Thank you for calling this to my attention. I will have Sue get together a team to deal with this. I also will let her know that she can expect your full cooperation. I am sure you will have no problem working for Sue on this one, since you are so concerned and are not able to work it out by yourself."

Having said how to deal with the obnoxious behavior, it is important to add the other side of the counter play. When the I-player does behave in acceptable and appropriate ways, treat him as you would anyone else. No, it is not a good idea intentionally to reward or reinforce acceptable behavior more so than with other staff. Appropriate behavior is to be expected, not rewarded. It is only necessary to reiterate that the I-player has to be treated like everyone else. Over time, he may come to behave more like everyone else, although this is unlikely. The only thing changing is the behavior of the people who have to deal with the player.

It will help to go back over the counter play in somewhat different terms. The I-player has—through whatever childhood and organizational experiences—come to believe that he is in important ways superior to and better than others. The result is that the player is used to receiving special consideration and deference. Within your company, his associates are being secondarily conditioned.

The process works like this: As most people interact with each other, each person does two things. First, he adjusts to and accommodates to others. Next, he projects his personality and style in a way that enables others to adjust to and accommodate to him. This process may be understood as reciprocal accommodation. For most people, the process quickly leads to a "fit" within the group.

The I-player neither understands nor functions within the reciprocal accommodation process. His social learning has taught him that he does not have to adjust to or accommodate to others. The player assumes that others will adjust to and accommodate to him. It simply never occurs to the I-player that it should work in the other direction too.

Enter the I-player into your group or organization. Even worse, enter someone new into your group or organization where the I-player is already entrenched. Most people, without thinking about it, try to adjust to and accommodate to the I-player. Since there is no reciprocity, the effort is all one-sided. Over time, people are bending over backward to get along with the player, and he assumes a special position and role. This reinforces the player's behavior and the game is on.

As an effective manager, you are alert to the game of the I-player and ready for counter play. The trick is to spot those relationships where the adaptation and accommodation are one-sided. When you see the pattern, the need is to treat the I-player the same as you treat everyone else. Do this by not adjusting or accommodating to him any more than to others. Your counter play indirectly gives permission to others in the group to follow your lead. Also, watch for and avoid any tendency to reinforce the I-player's perception of being better, smarter, more skilled, and more important than others.

Chapter Eight

Impersonal Players

ILLUSTRATION

Dr. Vincent Arnold is the Executive Director of the Pine Ridge Board of Mental Health and Mental Retardation. He finally has found time to catch up on his correspondence and to write a few notes to several of his associates. He prefers putting everything in writing for the record. For him, this is much better than talking with people directly and a good way to avoid those give-and-take discussions that sometimes are more like a free-for-all. It keeps things neat and orderly and allows for little variation from his view of how things should be. He is a believer in being precise and keeping everything under control.

TO: Jack

FROM: Vincent Arnold, Ph.D., Executive Director

RE: Your most recent correspondence

As a manager, I expect you to follow the system's policies and procedures completely and consistently. Based on your most recent report, I find you to be out of compliance with those policies and procedures.

The problems with the most recent version of the policies and procedures notwithstanding, I expect you to do what is necessary to bring your unit into compliance. Your belief that your unit has some differences from other units may have some validity. Nevertheless, it is your responsibility to be in compliance, regardless of what you may believe to be special circumstances. To make exceptions would serve only to undermine the efficiency and success of the system.

TO: Ronda

FROM: Vincent Arnold, Ph.D., Executive Director

RE: Your most recent correspondence

Because of my busy schedule, it will not be possible for me to meet with you and your group on the topic referenced in your correspondence at the time you suggested. I understand how important you believe this issue to be. I will have fifteen minutes to discuss it with you at 7:00 Thursday morning. Please have your comments organized so we may thoroughly cover the topic within the time allotted.

Specifically, two points will require complete clarification: (1) What role or part do you expect me to fill in the process? As Chief Executive Officer, I look to my assistants for guidance about these types of irregular involvements. (2) Your reference to "special needs" of your clients and what you call their "unique interests" are not at issue. These issues may be of clinical importance but are not matters of specific interest to administration. This is a business and must be operated as such. Special consideration, if it is to be given, must be managed at a client/therapist level. The primary responsibility of the MH&MR system is to be in complete compliance with the requirements of outside regulatory entities.

Please plan to address these points when we meet on Thursday.

TO: Staff Support Committee

FROM: Vincent Arnold, Ph.D., Executive Director

RE: Your most recent correspondence

I realize "morale" is always an area of complaint from the staff. Based on my experience, this is a personnel variable that fluctuates over time. In this instance, it is a product of necessary system changes and needs simply to be properly managed. Although it is important to take this into consideration, it may not interfere with the smooth and productive operation of the system. I have evaluated the current problem and believe it reflects the problems noted elsewhere with the managers. Also, many staff seem to be selfishly putting their feelings and perceptions on a par with or above the goals and interests of the system. The need is for all involved to put the problem into proper perspective and do what is necessary to accomplish the mutual objectives.

Please feel free to query me at any time about matters of concern to the committee.

TO: Malinda

FROM: Vincent Arnold, Ph.D., Executive Director

RE: Your most recent correspondence

This is to acknowledge your receipt of the Psychologist-of-the-Year award from the Psychological Association. This will be duly noted in your personnel record.

TO: James

FROM: Vincent Arnold, Ph.D., Executive Director

RE: Your most recent correspondence

Your request to have the policies waived in your case must be rejected. It is not good practice to make exceptions or give individuals special consideration. Although your request may seem reasonable from your perspective, it is not a concession that could be evenly applied to all employees.

Your argument that your years of experience with the MH&MR system should entitle you to special consideration in this instance is simply a request for favoritism. I am shocked you would attempt to impose on my position in that way.

I wish you success in developing a more satisfactory solution to your personal problem.

TO: Norma

FROM: Vincent Arnold, Ph.D., Executive Director

RE: Your most recent correspondence

Your correspondence was problematic on several accounts. First, the abrupt and threatening approach was inconsistent with the expectations and practices within the MH&MR system. Your lack of professionalism is unacceptable. A request must be stated as such and not put in the form of an order. I expect all employees regardless of rank or position to follow common rules of courtesy.

Second, your problems with the system computers are not of concern to me. I expect the data to be available on demand and expect you to do what is necessary to follow this policy. It goes without saying this must be done within the budget for your department.

Finally, your request for relaxation of the time and other expectations may not be considered. You seem not to understand the complex nature of the system and the demands placed on it. Relaxing one area has implications for the entire system. Each person must do his part as laid out in the ongoing planning process.

TO: Randy

FROM: Vincent Arnold, Ph.D., Executive Director

RE: Your most recent correspondence

As I previously communicated to you, the services of your department are unsatisfactory. Detailed explanations are not necessary. It is sufficient to inform you the services in question were transferred to the Emergency Service. This action is in the best interest of the MH&MR system. Further agitation on your part on this issue or persistent questioning of the decision will be counterproductive.

You will be well-advised to attend to the remaining services in your department. Be sure your staff is fully complying with all rules and regulations applicable to your operation. Smooth and effective functioning are the only issues of concern to you and your staff.

One implication of your correspondence warrants a specific comment. You state, by implication, the MH&MR Board and I deal with some programs, services, and people differently than others. We are proud of our record of even-handedness and treating all programs, services, and people alike. You may do well to follow the model being set for you.

DISCUSSION

The less astute observer may tend to confuse the Impersonal player with warriors, but you can see the important differences. The Impersonal player is a breed all his own.

The road to success with this method is to play with a total lack of interpersonal sensitivity. The trick is in maintaining a complete absence of any telltale signs of the social graces. It is *all business at all times.*

Dr. Arnold views the system as a machine and people and problems as annoying irrelevances. Consider for example, "The problems with the most recent version of the policies and procedures notwithstanding." The issues are always with the people and not with the instructions and most certainly not with the designer of the system. It is the function and purpose of people to behave in those ways defined by the designer—Dr. Arnold. Failure is always a problem of the people.

Part of carrying off the method is to be abrupt and too busy to get involved. For issues from minor to major, the effective player does not have time to deal with anything. He works it in later if absolutely necessary.

"Because of my busy schedule, it will not be possible for me to meet with you and your group. . . ." Of course, if there are problems later, the player's response is, "You should have consulted with me about this. You should have given more stress to its importance instead of bringing it up as a routine matter."

If the argument is, "I did stress its importance," the player responds, "The problem is you present everything as important. If you were a better manager and set priorities more carefully, you would not have this mess to work out."

Look at Dr. Vincent Arnold's clever way of discounting a problem. "I understand how important you believe this issue to be." For those who hear the words *you believe* and read between the lines, it is obvious that the good doctor does not think it is important at all.

The essence of his style goes even deeper, though. "I will have fifteen minutes to discuss it with you at 7:00 on Thursday morning. . . . Specifically, two points will require complete clarification."

Please play it back one note at a time for the thoughtful reader. The master makes it look like something perfectly reasonable. First, he makes it clear that no matter how important the problem, it only justifies fifteen minutes of his time. Score one for Dr. Arnold.

Next, he sets a time when no one wants to meet: 7:00 a.m. Score two for the doctor.

Next, he sets the agenda and requires a thorough presentation in fifteen minutes. Score another point for Vincent.

Here comes the capper. He demands that his two points receive complete clarification within the fifteen minutes. Is it just possible that there may be no time left to discuss the problem itself? Score a fourth for Dr. A. He pulls off a complete shutout. The problem will never get discussed.

Dr. Arnold also shows how a world class Impersonal player handles another tricky situation. Sometimes administrators are maneuvered into actions and behavior that are later criticized. To avoid this trap, it is necessary to put the responsibility for those actions onto others. Dr. Arnold needs to appear to be in charge while being able to dump off any repercussions onto his subordinates. It is good work if he can pull it off, and pull it off he can.

"What role or part do you expect me to fill in the process? As Chief Executive Officer, I look to my assistants for guidance about these types of irregular involvements." The small sleight of word "irregular involvements" is the key. Is it possible that any involvement with his staff is irregular? Sure. And any problems are due to the bad guidance he gets from his subordinates.

Dr. Vincent also shows there are other advantages attendant to positions at such heights as his. "Based on my experience, this is a personnel variable that fluctuates over time." From his perspective, Dr. Arnold is the best judge of staff issues. He best understands the problem, its causes, and the best response to the issues. That makes it easy. Everyone simply needs to quit complaining and get down to business, the doctor's business.

Whatever is going on with the staff is a system issue and need not be considered or dealt with in interpersonal terms. "People problems" only need to be managed and of course managed by someone other than the doctor. Given that other people do the managing for him, Vincent does not have to do anything. This gives him more time to further perfect his techniques.

"Also, many staff seem to be selfishly putting their feelings and perceptions on a par with or above the goals and interests of the system. The need is for all involved to put the problem into proper perspective and do what is necessary to accomplish the mutual objectives."

Dr. Arnold is not only an executive, he is a philosopher, perhaps even inspirational. Individual needs, feelings, and interests are subordinate to the goals and interests of the company as those goals and interests are defined by Dr. Vincent Arnold. This has the advantage that he never has to take anyone or anything into consideration beyond his needs, feelings, and interests. The outcome is eliminating any competition for the starring role, for the honored place at the center of the universe.

Throughout his implementation of the Impersonal-player methods and techniques, Dr. Arnold is consistent with the main requirement of the general method. He shows a total disregard for and disinterest in the human or feeling side of anything. The machine is central, and people are a necessary but not very important variable.

"This is to acknowledge your receipt of the Psychologist-of-the-Year award from the Psychological Association. This will be duly noted in your personnel record." The perfunctory way in which this individual matter is handled gives testimony to Vincent's complete mastery of *impersonal* technology. "This is to acknowledge" and "will be duly noted" are the clues to his play. The action is completely impersonal and may as well be handled by his assistant. In these days of computers and word processors, it can be handled as a form letter. This is a pure example of the "cold fish" technique.

Dr. Arnold can articulate his philosophy as system policy while including a flavor of condescending instruction.

"It is not good practice to make exceptions or give individuals special consideration."

Notice the policy: individuals do not get special consideration. Of course, this means that no one gets special consideration. As a rule, it could be stated, "Do everything by the book or pay the price." This is true even though "the book" is in a constant draft mode. The best part is that the book says whatever Vincent says it says today.

At another point in the illustration, Dr. Vincent Arnold succinctly explains the scope of his philosophy. "The primary responsibility of the MH&MR system is to be in complete compliance with the requirements of outside regulatory entities."

Now it is clear that his approach can be generalized. It can be applied to any organization having responsibility or accountability to some organization or entity outside itself. At a more micro level, it can also apply to any department within a larger organization. Only the naive think that the MH&MR system is primarily responsible for its staff. Only those who are totally out of touch with reality think that the primary responsibility is to the system's clients. A skilled player like Vincent Arnold never lets something as important as responsibility reduce to anything so human and unpredictable as staff or clients.

Perhaps the most subtle point is that Dr. Arnold is not the responsible party either. He is also subject to the outside regulators. Neat? It surely is. It lets everyone know that whatever he does, he is only following outside instructions. This makes him only incidental to the process.

By using this gambit, he has a process devoid of any concern about people—the goal of the ultimate Impersonal player. To be successful with his techniques, Vincent has to be sure others in the organization do not stray from the required pattern. At a minimum, people cannot deal with each other and especially not with him in emotional or irregular ways. Everything has to remain impersonal.

"Your lack of professionalism is unacceptable. . . . I expect all employees regardless of rank or position to follow common rules of courtesy." It is a parent saying to a child, "Never talk like that to me again. I demand respect and total deference. Do you understand, young man?" If anyone ever starts dealing with others as people or in feeling/emotional ways, Vincent's iron grip begins to slip. He is too good at being an Impersonal player to let this happen to him.

The range and depth of Dr. A's skills are mind-boggling. His ability to verbalize his approach in complete and comprehensive terms is inspirational. "Your request for relaxation of the time and other expectations may not be considered. . . . Each person must do his part as laid out in the ongoing planning process." This can be paraphrased as, "Your request will not even be considered because you are dumber than dirt." This is enough to dissuade even the most zealous associate from bringing problems or requests to Dr. Arnold.

There is also another subtle technique deserving attention. "As laid out in the ongoing planning process," is a classic example of The Frustration Factor. The message is, "As laid out in the plan that of course is continuously being revised." This makes it impossible for anyone to know what is expected. The plan is changing, and those who cannot keep up are out of luck. This takes "putting everything in writing" to a new level. The book can be rewritten without notice and is in typing if someone happens to have the last version. It is the moving target ploy. The motto is, "Always keep them guessing."

An extension of the guessing game comes with, "Detailed explanations are not necessary. . . . I have determined this action is in the best interest of the MH&MR system. Further agitation on your part on this issue or persistent questioning of the decision will be counterproductive." Asking questions is agitation and counterproductive, while explanations are superfluous. It sounds a lot like, "sit down and shut up." No one may question the actions of the king. It is like a game with unfamiliar and changing rules where the decisions of the self-appointed judge are final.

Consideration of the techniques and methods of Dr. Vincent Arnold concludes with a summary of his approach directly from his mouth to your ear. "We are proud of our record of evenhandedness and treating all programs, services, and people alike." It is a sign of the uninitiated to argue that programs, services, and people are different and should thus be treated differently. The experienced Impersonal player knows that this is the road to disaster. The trick is to keep the target moving, disregard the people, and never get personally involved. All things considered, Dr. Arnold may be a viable candidate for the player of the year award from FFSI.

IN BRIEF

Impersonal players think differences are unimportant

This technique is the essence of impersonal play. It applies to all people, situations, conditions, and circumstances. Each person in the organization is a replaceable production unit, and all events, conditions, and other aspects of operations are performance variables. The organization reduces to production and performance.

There are standards for production that the Impersonal player refers to often, and parallel standards for performance that are also liberally invoked. The trick is that these standards are subject to change without notice. They depend on the player's mood, the inclination toward or away from any specific person, department, or any other element the player happens on today. To the observer or participant, there may seem to be no rhyme nor reason, but the Impersonal player sees himself as totally evenhanded and objective. The key is nothing matters unless it happens to meet the fancy of the Impersonal player. The player says, "There are always two ways to do anything: my way and my way."

Impersonal players are impatient and in a hurry

This technique is self-explanatory but includes an interesting twist. Dr. Vincent Arnold might well include the following in one of his classic memos.

"I expect your report in my office by the close of business on Wednesday. I will review it and get back to you as soon as possible." As can be seen, the time rush applies to someone other than Dr. Arnold. The staff member has a deadline while Vincent will take his good old time. He is impatient and in a hurry with others but expects them to be patient and not to rush him. He is busier than anyone.

*Impersonal players do not clearly understand
their roles with people*

Players do well with charts, ongoing planning, lists of things to do, and time in their offices by themselves. Any time they are alone or have a program to let them know what to do, Impersonal players are in their elements. The problem comes when they need to "wing it" or "play it by ear." Then, people and conditions become idiosyncratic and unpredictable. The Impersonal player must avoid such uncertainty.

There are several ploys assuring the elimination of the unexpected and that prevent any direct need to deal with people. Requiring a detailed agenda is always good. This limits all interaction to topics and issues the player has rehearsed ahead of time.

Even better is having everyone talk while the Impersonal player listens and takes copious notes. "I will listen to the ideas of each of you and then take time to consider them. I will get back with you as soon after the meeting as practical."

The ultimate for the Impersonal player, though, is to bring an interpersonal type along to the meeting. The player sits quietly while the interpersonal type interacts. The best of the Impersonal players never goes to a meeting alone. He always takes his designated talkers.

As an added technique, if the Impersonal player is confronted in the hallway over anything, he suddenly has a meeting to which he is already late. The player has to have contingency plans for those times when people try to trap him into a discussion—or even worse—into a decision.

Impersonal players do not care about or understand the needs of others

Tim is a waiter at the Marietta Inn where he has worked for three weeks. It is Saturday evening and customers are standing in line to be seated. It has been that kind of night since about 6 p.m. Nothing is going right. Two of the suppliers are late with their deliveries, the head cook is out sick, and three servers did not show for their shifts.

Enter the Impersonal player. Bob Miller is only a little too loud and pushy about the wait in line. He is only somewhat more difficult when he and his party have to sit toward the back of the dining room. His real ability as a player does not come to the surface until Tim is trying to wait on Bob's party.

"I think having to wait twenty minutes to get in our orders is ridiculous. Is the service always this bad here?"

Tim is trying to be patient with Bob as he replies, "No sir. We've had a lot of problems tonight."

Not being one to back off from pressing his advantage, Bob says, "I don't think your problems are something I should have to suffer for. You should plan for times when things don't go exactly right."

Tim hangs in there as best he can. He says, "Thank you for your suggestion, sir. May I take your order?"

Not to be put off, Bob says, "Is dinner going to be as delayed as the service has been?"

Still under control, Tim says, "We will do our best, sir."

Once Tim serves their meals and leaves the table, one of Bob's dinner companions asks, "Weren't you a little rough on him, Bob? It does look like they have their hands full. If you come on like that in a restaurant, I'd hate to see you at work."

With a wide gesture and a smile, Bob says, "I have my own problems. I sure don't need to have other people dumping theirs on me, especially when I have a right to expect things to run smoothly."

Bob hates bad management, be it at a personal, department, or company level. Any variation from his standard is bad management and inexcusable. The needs or problems of people are but annoyances that must be eliminated. Bob is an Impersonal player of the highest order and may serve as a role model for the novice.

Impersonal players are always the best judges
of the environment

In the illustration, Vincent uses this technique effectively when he equates morale problems with staff complaints. The work environment is fine. Employees are merely complaining about problems that do not exist. This is true because the Doctor says it is true. The technique, however, may be applied in more innovative situations.

Ralph Zinn operates a jewelry store. He believes his customers want personal, private service. Following up on this belief, he divided the store into a show room and a viewing room. A customer browses in the show room and then completes a viewing request list. He notes items of interest and then goes to the viewing room. Items are then brought to him in a relaxed and private environment.

Ralph hired a public relations consultant to help improve his business. Enter the Impersonal player.

The Impersonal player, disguised as a consultant, knows a better way to do business. The viewing room becomes a storage room, and Ralph's store soon looks like a dozen others, glass cases, bright lights, crowds of people. But, customers who can afford what Ralph has to sell prefer the pampering, personal service, and special treatment they have come to expect. They are buying this as much as jewelry.

The story does not have a totally disastrous ending. Ralph's business only drops by twenty percent before he catches on. It drops another ten percent before he manages to send the consultant on her way and to put his store back the way it was.

Have no concern about the Impersonal player, though. She collects her $30,000, advises Ralph that the drop in sales is because of his lack of real sales expertise, and goes to her next engagement. It seems skilled players are never short of work.

*Impersonal players treat others differently
than they expect to be treated*

This is so axiomatic it hardly needs elaboration. If nothing else, Impersonal players always want and expect to be treated in special and deferential ways. Although the Impersonal player is skilled at excluding the human factor, he goes to extremes to be sure others do not relate in kind.

Dr. Arnold, in the illustration, schedules a fifteen minute appointment a few days away to be sure he is on someone's mind. At the restaurant, Bob makes sure Tim remembers him. In little and big ways, Impersonal players have a way of staying on your mind. They are there on your way home, at the dinner table, and even in your sleep, if you are one of their patsies.

Here is a little trick to spot experienced players. Over the next few days, make a mental record every time someone comes up in your thoughts or in your conversations with friends or co-workers. Now think about whether the thought or discussion is positive or negative. Counting only the negative, who comes up the most often? He may be an Impersonal player. Here is how to tell:

• Is he rigid and inflexible?

• Is he one of the last living people you would expect to be supportive of your activities, feelings, and goals?

• Does he have problems with give-and-take within relationships?

If you answer *Yes! Yes! Yes!* you have identified an Impersonal player.

Impersonal players do not think people need reasons or explanations

This technique comes in several forms. There is, "I am too far above you to warrant your receiving an explanation from me." This is the basic "snob trick."

At other times you see, "I am the boss and am not to be questioned," approach. This is the "high-and-mighty trick."

The next approach is, "I am too busy or important to take time to give you a reason or explanation." This is the "Buzz off! trick."

Additionally, there is, "You would not understand." This is the "You dumb . . . trick."

Finally comes the most common trick. "Don't ask for reasons or explanations when you already know quite well what the reason or explanation is." This is the "mind reader's trick." If you do not read minds, you are out of luck.

Whichever gambit he uses, the Impersonal player will carry it off with arrogance and style.

Impersonal players relate to everyone the same

This is the main technique required to be an Impersonal player. There are those "jerks" who are nice to some people and obnoxious with others, pleasant to your face, and then talk about you behind your back. Impersonal players are consistent and take pride in being evenhanded. They treat everyone equally badly, if it serves their purposes.

MANAGEMENT TIPS

Impersonal players are, in many ways, the most diffi-cult of all the people who drive you up the wall. They present unique counter play problems. They do not respond to differences in people or conditions. They attempt to handle everything and everyone in impersonal ways. Any relationship skills they may have are not especially useful in a traditional sense. Their impatience and lack of clarity about their roles compound the problems. They seldom take time to understand anyone or anything and do not intuitively or automatically see where they fit in or how their behavior affects others. They are confused but also confusing. This is additionally problematic because the player does not put people or their problems on his list of important concerns. Why? This is easy. The player is a know-it-all and does not have to come down to the people level.

Seeing this helps you understand the motivations of the Impersonal player. He is either incapable of or unwilling to think about things in human terms. He also believes that doing so is a less good or inferior way of interacting. With all this in mind the key to counter play is to deal with the player in impersonal and objective ways.

The first step is always to be calm and as rational as possible. Give the impression of not caring about things in any feeling or emotional way. Instead, convey a dispassionate but committed approach to things. Be a machine responding to another machine.

Whenever possible, put concerns in writing—or even better—present them directly but have a written report to pass along. This trick is important. The written presentation should not be more than one page long. For important or complex issues, longer reports are acceptable so long as they are not more than two pages. If it cannot be handled in two pages, think it through some more. The Impersonal player will only attend to the bare facts. Keep it short and to the point.

Finally, only include the specific problems, what is causing them, and exactly what is needed to fix them. Philosophy, how people are affected, or what people think about it are irrelevant. Focusing on them makes matters worse when dealing with the Impersonal player. Keep things short, factual, and free from people kinds of concerns.

It is helpful to think about the similarity between the Impersonal player and the I-player. The I-player does not participate in reciprocal accommodation. His lack of participation does not prevent others from trying to accommodate, though. For the Impersonal player, the process of reciprocal accommodation is irrelevant. Not only does the player not adjust or accommodate to others, he is unable to adjust to or accommodate to them in interpersonal terms.

The key to a relationship with an Impersonal player is to understand that there is not and cannot be any personal relationship.

Perhaps an analogy to a computer may help. When interacting with the machine, it is necessary to consider the output as literal. From the Impersonal Player, everything seen and heard must be taken literally and never in human or interpersonal terms.

Here is the most important part for you. Everything said to the player also must be literal. Only the empirical and objective are received and processed. The interaction is based on data and well-defined actions.

Finally and perhaps most importantly, the only way to reason with or influence the Impersonal Player is through input that has a direct impact on the player. Telling him how his actions or directives affect people or someone's operation is of no value. The computer has no interest in how its output impacts on people or situations.

Similarly, it has no ability to accept input that does not exactly match its program or expectations. Here is the key. The input has to be in a form that can be accepted. It must either be consistent with the computer's programming or such that it causes an error message in the computer. All input must either help the computer to run or threaten its operation.

Now counter play is clear. Take time to watch how the Impersonal player outputs information, instructions, and his expectations. Use the same medium and the same level of detail and exactness he uses. For example, in the illustration, those who want to deal with Dr. Vincent Arnold would do well to communicate in writing. The key is not to raise concerns and issues of others. Instead, it is better to say, "The staff morale problems are jeopardizing the ability of the Board to conform to regulations. Please advise."

Another example is, "Data processing irregularities are evident and attributable to the current equipment. The result is that external investigations may be anticipated. Please advise."

Just remember that the input must match the output. Keeping it impersonal is the road to success with the Impersonal player.

Chapter Nine

Agitators

ILLUSTRATION

The Rock Hill Community Church is a haven for agitators. Agitating is so much a part of church life that no one particularly notices anymore. There are several groups and cliques within the church, and observing some of them is illustrative of important techniques and methods.

Rev. O'Connor's sermon is especially lively for a Sunday in February. He moves quickly through social responsibility and the importance of brotherly love, right past helping one's neighbor and ministering to the needy, and into his point for the day.

"The real failing, my friends, is not to share in the pain and tribulations of our brothers and sisters. But it is worse to share in that pain and tribulation and then to elevate ourselves above the hurting by using the pain as a means of self-aggrandizement."

In an unusual gesture of consideration for those gathered to listen, Rev. O'Connor goes on to explain:

"I am talking about the gossips and busybodies, the talebearers and rumormongers. They are among us. Here, I do not exclude myself. I refer to those who fall to the low level of trying to seem in the know or important. This happens by taking pleasure in talking about or listening to conversations about the difficulties of others. Do we do this to be better able to lend a hand? Sadly the answer is "No." We do this to fill our own needs for attention and approval."

During the coffee hour after church, the small groups and cliques assemble in the social room. There are a few who mingle, but most take their usual places near their usual companions. A scattering of conversations can be overheard.

At a corner table, the preacher is the topic for the morning. "You should go to one of his so-called board meetings. All they do is gossip and waste time. If I were in charge, you can bet things would run better around here. We would take care of business and not spend all our time just sitting around getting nothing done."

In a small group toward the back of the social room, things are getting a little emotional. A teacher has just said, "I think I'm going to give up teaching one of these days. It's getting to where the children just have no respect. It was all right, but the new ones in the class just add to my problems. I don't know what has happened to the traditional family."

The group is sympathetic except for one young mother at the fringe. Abruptly, she sets down her coffee cup and rushes away.

The teacher says, "What got into her? She and her children have only been coming here for a couple of weeks, so I don't know her very well. Do any of you know her well enough to go see what she is upset about?"

The preacher is unaware of most of what is going on around the room. He is saying to an extremely animated man, "Melvin, I agree there is a problem. It may not be as bad as you think."

Not to be appeased, Melvin presses his point. "I don't think we should just brush this off as a minor problem. The next thing you know, the parents will be up in arms, and then the church itself may be in trouble. If we lose members over this, everything we've worked for will be in jeopardy."

Still trying, Rev. O'Connor says, "It's true Carolyn should not have said that to the child, if she said it. I will talk with her about what happened."

Just at the moment Rev. O'Connor thinks he has managed to get away from Melvin without getting him more upset, another agitator steps up. "I couldn't help hearing what Melvin said to you, Reverend. I don't want any bad feelings and wouldn't upset anyone for the world. I just have to say this. Carolyn is having family problems, and she deserves our support."

It is about twenty minutes later when the preacher feels a tug on his sleeve. As he turns, he hears, "I think you better talk with Carolyn. I think she has a right to hear it to her face. She is my best friend, and I'm going to stand by her."

Looking directly at Carolyn, Rev. O'Connor says, "I did not say anything about you to Melvin except you and I would talk. I would like to talk soon except this is not a good time or place. How about tomorrow sometime?"

With obvious sincerity, the friend says, "Carolyn does not need this hanging over her head." Turning to Carolyn, she says, "You are not going to let him put you off, are you?"

Unsure what to say, Carolyn says to the preacher, "So, what did Melvin say about me?"

As the preacher fumbles with what to say to Carolyn, the agitator says, "I can see this is getting a little personal. If the two of you don't mind, I will be headed home. I have a hungry family to feed. I will call you later, Carolyn."

DISCUSSION

The illustration covers about forty-five minutes on a Sunday morning. Imagine the chances to experience other agitators had you stayed around for a day or a week.

The illustration shows the stock and trade of the agitator. It is having information—being in the know without a high level of importance placed on accuracy or relevance.

For example, you can imagine one of the gossips asking, "Do you know what was going around about him last year?"

Curiosity may have killed the cat, but it is the main bait of the agitator. Not many can resist responding, "No, what?"

Now the player can tell all, with little if any concern for truth or relevance. Anyway, the player never says it is true. It is just something that was going around—and is now going around again, thanks to the player.

The ambitious player learns to embellish and shape the information to increase its importance. An effective way of doing this comes from Melvin. "I don't think we should just brush this off as a minor problem." Melvin is exceptional. Carolyn says something to one child. Consequently, the church itself is at risk. With the church at risk, Melvin has no difficulty getting almost anyone to listen and take him seriously.

Along with the ability to amplify the information, the successful player has a real knack for turning any conversation in negative and problematic directions. The way the church member talks about the board meetings is an instructive example of agitating. It is easy to miss the smooth way the player chains several techniques.

First, the player represents Rev. O'Connor as an example of something undesirable, someone who tells people not to gossip and then does that very thing at his board meetings.

If that is not enough, the preacher is dishonest and pulls the wool over everyone's eyes except the player's. He does this at his so-called board meetings. "So-called" is the key to the ploy. They are not proper board meetings at all. The agitator exposes the fraud.

Now comes the closer. "If I were in charge. . ." Of course the player is not and will never be in charge. The long and short of what the player says is, "I am more competent than the preacher." This is why others should listen to him and listen they do.

The chief element in the play is this. As the player talks to his buddies, the message is that they too are more competent than the preacher. The player takes the high status role and offers similar roles to his friends. Most all behavior that drives you up the wall reduces to the acquisition and distribution of power and influence. People are trying to gain or protect power or perceived power.

The teacher in the illustration gives you an especially cruel example of the method. Her clever gambit comes when she splits her play into two parts. First comes, "It was all right but the new ones in the class just add to my problems." After the young mother sets down her coffee cup and rushes away, the agitator asks, "What got into her?"

Suppose another member of the group suggests that the teacher upset the woman. The teacher acts shocked and says, "I have no idea what you are talking about. I was not talking about her and her children." It matters little anyway. The mother and her children likely will not be back so the player will never have to deal with the outcome of her behavior. It is a variation of the hit-and-run play, except here it is hit and the other person runs.

There is yet another agitator getting in her two cents worth whether anyone wants to hear it or not. "I do not want any bad feelings and would not upset anyone for the world. I just have to say this." Of course, she knows there will be bad feelings and someone will get upset. The trick is to deny any intent although the player well-knows what is going to happen. It is like saying, "I would not hurt you for anything," and then punching the person in the nose.

Having given a disclaimer of any malicious intent, the player says, "I just have to say this." She does not want to but has to say it. Maybe the devil is making her do it.

What if someone interrupts and says, "No, you do not have to say anything."

The player then says, "I'm sorry, but I do have to say it. It has to be said." Only the totally unsocialized refuse to back off and let her say her piece. Sooner or later the agitator takes center stage with a receptive audience.

There is one last complex gambit. It starts with, "I think you better talk with Carolyn. . . . I think she has a right to hear it to her face." This opens the interchange on just the right note for the agitator. The preacher is immediately on the defensive, and the player is ready for the assault. The stage is set.

The preacher tries to put it off but the agitator has none of that. "I think we should settle this now."

The player presses on in spite of the preacher's efforts to calm the troubled waters. "You are not going to let him put you off, are you?" If Carolyn says, "Yes," she is a patsy and someone who lets others kick her around. If she says, "No," the confrontation is inevitable. Most people do the face-saving thing and say, "No, I will not be put off like that." It is human nature that helps the player succeed.

The closer for the gambit is when the real stroke of genius comes. "I can see this is getting a little personal. . . . I will be headed home." The player creates the scene, encourages the participants, and sets the stage for the confrontation. Her work is done. On cue, she exits and lets the scene play itself. Her motto is, "Why don't the two of you go fight?"

This agitator is an experienced player. How can you tell? Players with less experience usually stay to watch.

With experience, they learn that the risk of watching is that the combatants may join forces and turn on the player, if he is still there. The trick is to set the stage and then get as far away as possible.

IN BRIEF

Agitators tell all to anyone

To master this technique, it is necessary to keep in mind that the underlying motivation relates to the acquisition and distribution of power and influence. To get power or influence, the player tells anything to anyone. The trick is that this seems also to give more power or influence to the person receiving the information. Another example will help here.

Alice Noris is the Projects Director for a small electronics company. In her position, she is a confidante to the executive vice president and occasionally to the president. She also uses her position to become friendly with the operations director of the company's largest customer. Due to a corporate reorganization, Alice is being laid off and becomes quite bitter. Her main problem is losing her base of power and influence.

For a couple of weeks, Alice flounders, not knowing how to deal with what is a revolting predicament. Her inspiration, however, soon comes.

Alice takes a double tack. First, she spends some time hanging around the company, *just visiting with her friends.* Second, she actively pursues her relationships with her "friends" from the company's customer. Along with the information she already has through her employment, she gets more rumors and tidbits of information from hanging around. These arrangements put her in an ideal position to play out her power game.

Her first ploy is to intimate to the company's remaining employees that the company is going down the tube. This is, of course, because she is not going to be there anymore. This has the effect of getting the employees upset and anxious about their jobs.

To the customer's staff, she gives the impression that the company is poorly managed and in big trouble. This undermines the customer's faith in the company and its willingness to contract with Alice's ex-employer.

The message to both circles of "friends" is that if Alice were in charge, things would be running smoothly. Of course, both groups of people are interested in the *inside information*. It puts them in the know. Alice gains more power and influence within both groups of confederates. Having the scoop always equates with having power.

Agitators get others upset and then act innocent

This is the "Who me?" trick and is a technique only for the very skilled. It plays out in two ways, sometimes mixing the approaches.

First, pick something the other person highly values or finds a little problematic for him. This can be anything from a personal quality or attribute to an aspect of work performance or a specific task. The key is to be sure it is important, valued, or a point of concern to the person. This then becomes the target.

Second, pick a person liked by the individual or someone whose opinion the person values. Playing it straight up, get the valued other to say something negative about the person related to the target trait or situation. If a skilled player listens closely, something can be given a negative twist even if nothing negative was intended.

Using the first ploy, the player says something to his foil directly. Using the second ploy, he says something to his victim, attributing the comment to the valued other. An example of each technique is instructive.

Using the direct approach, Nancy finds an opportunity to chat with one of her co-workers. "This is something I would never say to you if we were not such good friends. I just feel like I have to tell you the truth. Please stop me if you don't want me to be honest with you. Well anyway, I saw that program you wrote for the Market Center account. Granted, it gets the job done. How to say this? It is a little convoluted. I just thought you should know there were better and cleaner ways to write the code."

Her co-worker asks, "Like what?"

Nancy smiles and says, "I should not have brought it up. You are going to do nothing but get upset. We are too good friends to have hard feelings over something like this. Just pretend I didn't bring it up. Let's talk about something else."

Why does Nancy bring it up at all? That is the remarkable part of it. No one will ever know but Nancy what it had to do with her short-term or long-term game plan, but be assured that Nancy knows. Agitators are always aware of what they are doing and why they are doing it.

Nancy also is skilled with the indirect approach. She just happens to be talking to Jeff Mallary, the manager of her operating unit. Mary—the above co-worker—just happens to come up in the conversation. "It's interesting you should mention Mary, Jeff. I was talking with her earlier today about the problems with the program she wrote for the Market Center account. It's too bad I didn't get to see the code before it went out. It might be a good idea if I reviewed her stuff before it goes out to catch these kinds of things before they get to our customers. Two heads are always better than one. How would something like that seem to you, just to be on the safe side?"

"Well, it sure can't hurt anything, if you have the time," is Jeff's offhanded reply.

Later the same day: "I talked with Jeff, Mary, and he is upset about the problems with the Market Center project. He asked me to supervise your programming activities and to approve everything before it goes out. With our being such good friends, I assured him this would not cause any problems."

Agitators are quick to complain

Most of the techniques have been demonstrated by master players as in the above examples. This one is for beginners, though.

Suppose you want to advise someone how to be an agitator. It might go like this:

- Start with people higher up or with the work of people in other departments

- Pick a person or problem to focus on

- Once over the selection hurdle, systematically avoid saying anything about the person or problem unless saying something negative

- Be sure to say something negative every time a chance to agitate comes up

- Take care to say something negative about the performance of the person or something about how the problem is being poorly handled

- "If it were up to me," is always a good opener when using the technique.

So long as the aspiring agitator takes care to limit the technique to one or two people or situations, it is hard to go wrong. With everyone and everything else, the new player needs to at least be noncommittal and should be downright positive at times. This gives the impression of being a positive person who is a team player.

Agitators make things seem worse than they are

The corollary to this is that agitators also make things that are quite positive seem less positive. When the two sides of the technique are seen—worse and less positive—it is easier to get a feel for how to play.

Someone says, "Charlie did a fine job."

The player responds, "Yes, he did do all right this time." All right, but not quite a fine job.

Alternatively, someone says, "Charlie had some problems with that one."

The player responds, "I suppose it could have been worse, but he for sure didn't get the job done."—"Some problems" change to "could have been worse" and "not get the job done."

The idea is to move it just a little in the negative direction whether it starts out positive or starts out already negative.

Agitators have opinions on everything

This technique is the stock-in-trade of the effective agitator. His trick is to use the technique in a skilled and unexpected way. The player puts in his two cents worth at every opportunity, whether anyone wants it or not. It works like this.

Rose hangs around when others are talking, always lingers a little after meetings, and just starts talking when people are working. Her game is to get people talking whether they want to talk or not.

Once people are talking, she jumps in or says something like, "I could not help hearing what you were talking about." Of course, she could help it. She makes a point to hear. Nonetheless, she now expresses her opinion. Whatever the topic, she has an opinion.

Her opinion is that things are a mess. She thinks things should be handled better. In fact, the company is going to the dogs. Why? Everyone—except her—is incompetent and does not know what he is doing. Adding, "I have said this before but. . . ." is a master touch.

Here is the key to the technique. If someone asks Rose for her opinion on something, she says, "I have some strong opinions on this, but I want to hear your ideas first." Notice she is clear about her having opinions—more than one—on the topic. No matter what the other person says, Rose is ready. She has managed to move back to a position from which to react to what others are saying. She is not one to let anyone get her out of position. The thorn of Rose works best as a weapon with which to stick someone, anyone.

Agitators keep things stirred up

Effectively using this technique is a difficult task. The need is to keep things stirred up without being seen as an agitator. The player needs to play without being identified as an agitator. Success comes by being able to strike when it will stir things up the most and being perfectly charming the rest of the time. The impression is of a likeable person who only has the best interest of your company at heart. He only says anything at all because he sincerely cares.

There are many effective ways and times to get to the goal of stirring things up. The two best times are either when things are going along smoothly or when stress and tension are unusually high. The rest of the time, the player needs to be charming.

There also are two good ways to get things stirred up. First, when things are going well, find a little problem and predict that it will grow into a crisis. Sooner or later there will be a crisis of some sort. The player can then say, "I wish I had been wrong, but I tried to warn you." It does not matter if the original problem had anything to do with the current crisis. The player is a *big person* in the scheme of things as a result of predicting the crisis. People now hold him in higher regard.

When things are a mess or when there is a crisis, the player picks anyone or anything on which to blame the problems. It helps to select someone or something others already see as a problem, but it does not really matter.

The player says, "As I have pointed out before, our real problem is. . . ." No, it does not matter whether it is the problem or if it has been pointed out before. Everyone will feel better having someone or something on which to focus their frustration and negative energy. The player finds a scapegoat for them. Nearly everyone would rather point fingers than deal with the real issues. How about that! Human nature again works to the player's advantage.

MANAGEMENT TIPS

Understanding the motivations of agitators is not too difficult if you look at their behavior and then ask yourself why they are behaving that way. More to the point, what do they get out of it? Their motivations are in the payoff or what they get.

The agitator will say anything no matter who gets hurt or feels badly. What does the player get? He gets a cheap moment in the spotlight, even if it is at the expense of a co-worker. Just keep in mind that the player will say anything about anyone, including you. The agitator also gets his kicks from complaining. He is again in the spotlight. Of course, there is always a little more power in that position.

The player makes things seem bad, people seem incompetent, and everything appears worse than it is. The player gets attention, gets a little more power for a little while, and is seen as someone who is in the know and on top of things. Experienced players do this in a way that grows over time. They also take care not to overdo it. They are very good at not giving away their game.

Given the behavior, its varieties and its motivations, what does counter play look like? Listen to what the agitator has to say and then say, "You are a trip. You can find more ways to look at things negatively than anyone I know." The strategy is to call the player on his behavior and make it clear that you have no interest in what he says. There is no power reinforcement for the behavior.

In another example, a player is agitating. He says something negative about someone. The classy response is, "I am surprised to hear you say that. I do not think it is true." The player will almost always press on with, "It is true! I . . ." He goes on to say some more negative things.

Your response is, "You probably would describe the tooth fairy as a thief." Now comes the real trick. No matter what the player says next, do not respond. The game is over.

As with most people who drive you up the wall, the trick to counter play with agitators is to do what needs to be done and then quit. Players of any type or variety can only play with people who will play. For agitators, just be sure they get minimal attention and no additional power or status from you. Quietly and calmly call them on their behavior and then let it go. When others do not play, the game gradually stops.

Also when agitating gets started in a group, it tends to be contagious. The play is hard to resist. People who just enjoy small talk—almost always about other people who are not there—inadvertently pick up the behavior. The play becomes a way to get status and attention in the group. It works for the agitator so why not for others?

Given the contagious virility of the game, it is important to stop it as quickly and completely as possible.

Locate the most vocal agitator and then do two things: First, privately ask him to tell you what problems he sees or what concerns he has. If necessary, candidly share with him what you have learned he is saying or complaining about. Once the issues are on the table, you and he can go into a problem solving mode.

Next, and this is the key, tell him that his agitating behavior is unacceptable. Let him know that you are always available to work on problems but will not tolerate agitating. He will undoubtedly act shocked and deny the behavior. Nonetheless, make your point and do not argue with him.

If necessary and after giving problem solving a chance, say to the player, "This behavior must stop. If not, I will call a meeting of the group. At that time, I will again say to you that your destructive behavior must stop. I also will caution your associates not to follow your example."

This is usually enough. You must not be bluffing, though. It may be necessary for you to follow through, especially with dyed-in-the-wool agitators.

Chapter Ten

Negotiating With Advanced Players

INTRODUCTION

You are now familiar with the methods and techniques of people who drive you up the wall and are becoming skilled at counter play. It is now time to extend your skills into what will likely be a most exciting arena for you—negotiations.

The approach here is to highlight individual techniques used by advanced players, by people who drive you up the wall. Next, you see examples of experienced players in negotiating contexts. You then will receive tips and suggestions for successful counter play.

TECHNIQUES IN BRIEF

Players demand things the other party neither has nor controls

This is one of the most effective negotiating techniques available to the skilled player so long as the demand is not too far-fetched or outrageous. Even then, the experienced player can go further than you may first think.

Bryan is negotiating with his boss about whether Bryan stays with the company or accepts a lucrative offer from a competitor.

Bryan says, "Money is not all there is to this. I will have to get just a few concessions to stay. I feel a lot of loyalty to this company. I need a larger office and a secretary and, well, having a nicer company car would help things at home. I will need to sell Carol, my wife, on turning this other deal down. Here's the main thing. I have to have the freedom to go with project ideas without going through all the hassle and committees to get something off the ground. You know it takes more time and energy around here to get an idea through the system than it does to try it. I have to have a free hand in my area."

His boss reacts, "Even I don't have that kind of latitude. I couldn't give that to you even if I thought it was reasonable and I'm not sure I do. We need some checks on what happens around here. Get real Bryan! Let's talk about the other things, but the kind of latitude you are asking for is out of the question."

Note the boss's use of the "flinch" technique. Someone might think he is actually shocked by Bryan's request for a "no prior approval" deal.

Bryan waits a long time before continuing. He then says, "We can talk about the other things and see how it goes with them. But you need to understand that creative freedom is a high priority for me. It has to come back on the table at some point."

Note the use of the "set aside" technique by Bryan. "Creative freedom" is set aside for now.

With a noticeably more eager approach, Bryan's boss says, "I can handle that. Let's get into the office and car issues and see if we can make you happy." With a little laugh, he adds, "How would Carol like a new Buick?"

Way to go Bryan! What is a little creative freedom when compared to a bigger office, a new car, and a few other things your boss may just throw in to keep you off your outrageous demand kick? Who knows? He may even throw in a little more creative freedom just to close the deal.

The boss falls into the trap. He does not deal with the outrageous demand as one demand on a list of equal demands. Instead, he puts it on one side of the ledger as a "not over my dead body" issue. The other demands then seem minor and reasonable in comparison.

Better would have been for the boss to say, "Let's make a list of your demands: a new car, a bigger office, more creative freedom, ..."

Notice that the outrageous demand only makes third place. Also it changes from "complete freedom" to "more freedom." If Bryan objects, the boss can focus attention on what should go on the list and how they should be stated. As a skilled manager, the boss keeps focus on the list and not on any single demand.

Players demand things the other party has
but cannot concede

Using this technique is in the same league as demanding something the other party does not have. In fact, it is a little better in some ways. Suppose in the example above, Bryan's boss has the authority to give him a complete waiver of pre-approval requirements. His bind is that he has already refused to give that kind of latitude to a couple of other people who have been with the company longer than Bryan. If he gives it to Bryan, he will be in an impossible predicament. Two of the others appealed his decision to his boss. Bryan's boss has taken a lot of heat and would be hard put to make it through that again. If he meets Bryan's demand, he is likely to lose the power battle that the other employees will start.

This time Bryan says, "Your trust and confidence in me will be a big part of my final decision. Creative freedom is more than just a perk or something trivial like offices and cars. It gets at our working relationship, our friendship. It is that simple. Either you trust me or you don't. All you have to do is say yes or no."

Smooth move Bryan! You now have control. Your boss now has to prove to you he is a sincere guy who trusts you. It may be good for at least a few more options on Carol's Buick.

Bryan has used a spurious argument and the boss must not play. He has equated "creative freedom" and "trust." Whether he is trusted or not, the skilled manager stops that process cold.

The boss can say, "Give me a break. I'm surprised you would try such a cheap shot. You know as well as I do the project approval process is a matter of company policy. It serves to let all departments comment on how the project will work with their operations. You are too sophisticated to pull that emotional stuff with me. Let's talk about what the real issues are."

The boss has obviously been there before. Calling Bryan's creative freedom the "project approval process" is just the right touch. Also, he uses Bryan's own trick on him. Now Bryan has to back off a little or tacitly admit to not being sophisticated. It appears that the boss is back in control.

Players do not concern themselves
with the cost to them of having their demands met

Countering this technique is particularly dangerous for all but the expert manager. Suppose Bryan's boss decides to cave-in and give Bryan exactly what he demands?

His Boss says, "Bryan, you are one in a thousand and you know it. I just can't afford to lose you, especially not to the competition. There will be no pre-approval requirements."

Without a further thought, Bryan accepts the offer saying, "Get it written up and I will sign it."

Bryan does not concern himself about the contract's tying all salary increases and some new performance penalties to the success of his projects—the cost of having his demands met. He is up to the arrangement whatever the cost. Instead of pursuing truly creative but risky projects, he moves to a modified game of B-t-B. Never mind what he might have accomplished had he hit on one of those more risky ideas he now so carefully avoids. Bryan's priority is to take care of Bryan, to take no chances.

The skilled manager first needs to see that his responsibility is to the welfare and well-being of the company. This means two questions must be answered before making any offer. Is the arrangement being offered to the employee in the company's best interest? The deal made with Bryan likely is not. Next, is it consistent with the existing arrangements with other employees? It is important that it is not and does not appear like a "sweet deal" for one person only. The problems that causes with other employees are almost never worth it. The boss will pay dearly for the sweet deal made with Bryan, sooner or later.

A skilled manager sees the equally important issue as well. He always asks, "Will this work to the employee's advantage over time? Will it increase his productivity, satisfaction, and over-all success?"

Unless the answers to these questions are "Yes," do not make the offer, even though the employee may accept it. The arrangement made with Bryan eliminates the possibility of his being as successful as he potentially may be. One of these days, he will figure that out and will again become restless and discontented. The sweet deal will not hold up over time. Bryan will eventually figure out that the cost to him is too high.

Players overvalue those points on which they
and the other party might agree

Watch how the boss tries to use this technique on Bryan. Bryan makes the same pitch. Instead of responding to the "creative freedom" issue, his boss says, "I respect and appreciate your sense of loyalty to the company and value your dedication over the years. There is a glitch or two, but I can and will give you almost everything you want. We have worked together long enough; we think alike. Any time we agree on 95 percent of the issues, a contract is easy."

Bryan's boss then lists the areas of agreement and says, "It looks to me like we have a contract. Isn't that the way you see it?"

Not this time, boss! Bryan will not be taken in with that old ploy. The game is to give the impression that all that remains are a few loose ends.

Bryan says, "I wish I could set aside the creative freedom issue, but it is too important to brush aside. It may be the only thing we do need to talk about."

The boss tries to make it seem like they have a deal, but Bryan knows that he needs to press on what he has not yet gotten. Acknowledging too much convergence—points of agreement—is a quick way to lose out, as Bryan knows. He is not someone who can be seduced so easily.

The boss tries again, making everything dependent on everything else. This means the negotiation starts afresh.

The boss says, "I would have liked to work some of these things out first and then deal with others later. We can go with your approach, though, if you are most comfortable with it. I can give you most (not 95 percent any more) of what you want. Working this out with you is important to me. Also, I can give you any single item under certain conditions. Let's talk about each item and about what will be important conditions. Which item do you want to start with?"

Players do not think areas of difference
or disagreement are particularly important

This is a clever technique. In essence, the ploy means it does not matter if the player and the other party agree on anything at any point in time. It is always possible to find something.

"Well, I guess we can at least agree we don't seem to agree on much. That is a place to start. Let's list our points of disagreement to see if we can agree on what all goes on the list. Can we agree on that as a place to start?"

At a more advanced level, no acknowledgment at all is made of any divergence—points of disagreement. For example, Joyce Allen is a nurse at a sixty bed convalescent home for the elderly. She and another nurse are responsible for the guests on one wing of the home. Their problem is how to best divide the duties to be sure all guests receive proper care.

The other nurse says, "We have some serious problems here. Our philosophies of care and work patterns are worlds apart and causing more work for both of us. We need to come to some compromise about these disagreements so we can both do our work."

Acting a little surprised, Joyce says, "It's not a big deal. We are both nurses and want quality care for our patients. At the core, we both know how to do our jobs and have to keep our patients as our primary concern."

Her associate then mentions a couple of things she sees as problematic. Joyce just smiles and says, "Hey, we stumble over each other a little, but that is to be expected. It does not bother me. In fact, it gets a little humorous at times. We're both good nurses and need to keep our senses of humor and keep on being professional about how we deal with our patients, as we both always do. The problems are just one of those things."

Joyce is a master at driving people up the wall and is going to continue her previous behavior. Perhaps, her associate will get frustrated and quit. That can give Joyce a new person to start her play with all over again.

A skilled manager sees through the game. The idea is never to deal with the problems. This enables the player to avoid any effort or energy required to adjust or accommodate. You can see the absence of reciprocal accommodation.

For the player, the goal is to have others adjust to him. If they do not, it is of no concern or interest to the player.

Here is one way to deal with the problem. Use a well-worded response like this: "It is unfortunate you think serious professional issues are humorous. I doubt our patients (use the clinical term) see their care as a joke. There are other ways to deal with quality of care issues like this, but I prefer to resolve them directly with you. Would you prefer that approach or more formal procedures?" At least the player must now take the differences more seriously.

Players take positions on which they are intransigent, positions that are their bottom lines

This is a technique only used by organizational high rollers. It is a crapshoot with what the player believes to be loaded dice.

Suppose the other nurse says to Joyce, "This may not seem like a big deal to you. For me, it is a matter of principle (a typical reason for hanging tough). I am going to have to see some changes. . . ."

Notice the unspoken threat. The unsaid threat is, "If I don't see some changes, I will do something you will not like."

The task for Joyce is to weigh the cost of changing her behavior against the likelihood and cost of the other person's following through with the threat. Joyce has come up against another skilled player. The trick for the other nurse is to be sure she can make the stakes high enough. If Joyce is not immediately intimidated, a good play might be for her to say to Joyce, "I'm serious, Joyce. This is a bottom line issue for me. I don't think either of us would relish taking this through peer review but. . . ." Perhaps even a player like Joyce may give a little over this one. If she does not, the other nurse need only raise the stakes next time. The best thing is that she need never follow through. She need only use the technique sparingly and with sincerity and a high level of credibility. The only need is for Joyce to believe.

In this example, the play is all power: capitulate to me or I will find a bigger stick to hit you with. There is no back up or negotiating position.

The task for the skilled manager is first to refrain from reacting emotionally. The response must be reasoned. An appropriate response is, "You seem to be threatening me. I hear you saying to do things your way or you will figure out a way to sabotage my work and perhaps my career. Your lack of professionalism is amazing."

Pick neither fight nor flight. Pick the strategies of the skilled manager.

Players think people negotiate
based on shared goals and values

This is a useful technique used by beginners since most people buy in up-front. In other words, most people believe that when people are negotiating, they have the same goals and values. The negotiations are, they think, over details or specific provisions.

The teachers and the school board are in contract negotiations. The board's negotiator says, "In this case, it is not like most negotiations. Here, we are all on the same side. We all want the same things—the best possible education for the children. We want a secure situation for the teachers and a sound financial environment for the board; but most of all, we want what is best for the children."

Later in the process, you can hear her saying, "If the board's financial position becomes unstable, we all suffer; but most importantly, the children suffer. Avoiding harm to the children is something to which I know we are all committed, aren't we?"

It is easy to get a feel for the ploy. First, the player establishes the shared value—the welfare of the children. In other situations, this could be patriotism, motherhood, or maybe even apple pie. The point no one will raise because it might be read as unprofessional is that the negotiations have nothing to do with the welfare of the children. They are negotiating about the welfare of the board and the welfare of the teachers. So long as the player can keep the focus on the children as a shared goal and value, though, she has a lever. Any time things get rough, she can say, "Let's get back to what we all agree is important here—the welfare of the children."

Probably no one will say, "Get off it! We are talking about dental coverage and not about the goodness of children. Our people need and deserve a $50 deductible here and are insulted by this $100 stuff you keep pushing."

When push comes to shove, people will do the polite and professional thing. The player is counting on it.

The skilled manager uses two approaches here. They are not complex but depend on being able to spot and understand the game. First, call the player on the game. You might say, "Let's stop for a second to think through a little point. We all agree we are here to do the professional and ethical thing. The children and their education are of high value. Using references to that important issue here, though, does not serve us well and is insulting. Let us not debate who cares the most. We all care."

Next say, "Having agreed that the children are important, let's not use them. Can we all agree that we will not use the "who-cares-the-most" tactic to make our points or to counter the points of the other side? Can we agree to keep our attention on the important issues before us?"

What happens if the who-cares-the-most ploy is again used? Sit back, smile, and use the words of one of our past presidents, "There you go again."

Players are likely to devalue their hands

This is a *Little-Red-Riding Hood* and *The Big-Bad-Wolf* technique. Little Red Riding Hood is the player in the scene. Look at how it works.

Little R-R puts herself out there in the woods where no one but big-bad-wolves should ever go alone. Any 1990s woods walker with half a brain would go prepared and ready to deal with wolves, big, bad, or not. Not R-R, though. She just strolls along, counting on her ability as a player.

As expected, B-B-Wolf walks up to R-R and says, "I am going to have you for lunch!"

R-R says, "Oh please sir! I am a poor little thing and am on my way to see my grandmother who is on her death bed. Please do not take advantage of me."

Being a polite wolf who wants to do the right thing, B-B says, "I do not want to take advantage of a weak little thing like you. I will give you safe passage this time. Please do not go out in the woods by yourself any more."

Sure, R-R will follow B-B's advice, at least until the next time she gets caught out by herself.

You see R-R and B-B in many situations. Negotiations are a frequent background for the scene. It comes in little and large, direct and indirect ways. The player asks for special consideration, concessions, unusual privileges or exemption from the normal consequences. This should happen because of the player's being new, inexperienced, not as skilled, or outclassed. Whatever the excuse, the message is, "You should not abuse or take advantage of me." Sure, it is a new application for "Poor-Me."

How does the skilled manager deal with the R-R syndrome? It is easy to take the position that "it is a jungle out there," and anyone who cannot take care of himself is out of luck. The problem is that there are those who get into negotiations without the skills or experience needed to participate on an equal footing.

The skilled manager first determines whether the other person is up to the negotiation. If not, he suggests—and at times insists—that the other party brings in a qualified negotiator before the process continues. At a minimum, he avoids knowingly taking advantage of the other person.

B-B-Wolf has the right idea. He refrains from the kill and sends R-R on her way, suggesting that she better come prepared next time. If she does not, B-B-Wolf needs to develop more effective ways to get R-R to take care of herself. Whatever the outcome, B-B-W will not be the one to take advantage of her, no matter how tempting.

The skilled manager makes sure there is a real inability or disadvantage, though. Careful attention is given to assuring it is not a game run by an expert Poor-Me player.

Players agree to conditions or considerations
they cannot honor

Use of this technique makes negotiations much easier for the player than they might otherwise be. The trick is to only use the technique for things that do not have to be delivered up front. The play is for things coming later like complete performance on the contract.

Consider further the teacher/board negotiations. Suppose the board has two general concerns. First, the test scores for the school are below average when compared to national averages. Second, the board wants to have some way of assuring its teachers are competent.

The board negotiator says, "We want the second and third year salary increases contingent on an improvement in test scores. We also want to institute competence testing for all teachers in the system."

The teachers' negotiator says, "These are both worthy goals and are in the interest of the welfare of our students. We support and applaud this kind of forward thinking. We are pleased to put them on the table here today."

It is such a good idea that the teachers' negotiator takes credit for it—for the welfare of the children, you may assume.

Note how the teachers' negotiator makes test scores and competence of the teachers a goal and not an ironclad guarantee. Having made the semantic switch, he says, "We will agree to anything reasonable in these areas. We are ready to agree today to form a board/teacher task force to establish the guidelines and specific rules to reach these worthy goals. It would be the charge of the task force to have its final report within six months for inclusion, by mutual agreement at that time, into this contract. Can we agree to sign off on this today to assure quality education for our children?"

If the board's negotiator says, "Then you are agreeing to have the second and third year increases contingent on the task force findings?" The player goes for round two.

He says, "The teachers agree. Of course, just as the board cannot predict what the findings will be, neither can the teachers. We need a contract by the end of the week, so the teachers want a penalty provision or waiver if the task force does not get its job satisfactorily completed."

Note the use of the "drop dead" technique: a contract by the end of the week.

Rounds three and four may be even more interesting. The key is that the player agrees to anything, so long as it does not have to be done today. Agreement is even quicker, so long as it never becomes an up-front condition for something else. It is a "nice-work-if-you-never-have-to-do-it" kind of thing.

Players press to get all their demands met

This is a "wear them out" technique and is only for those with unusual patience and endurance. For the player with these qualities, however, the technique is powerful.

The teachers' negotiator puts the end of the week as a drop dead point in the negotiations. Suppose the board's negotiator says, "If we have to have this wrapped up by the end of the week, I commit to having meals delivered. We can stay here around the clock until we get this worked out. We can form the task force right now and call in anyone who needs to be here. We can stay at it until we get what we need for both the test scores and the competency rules. At the same time, we can come to closure on the rest of the board's needs. The board cannot let go of this until we have an agreement on each point."

Notice how she circles back to pick up the board's interests and demands. No matter how much agreement develops, the board's negotiator keeps everything on the table. Her hope is that sooner or later the board will get most everything it wants.

The real trick is that the board will get a few things just because the other side becomes bored, exhausted, frustrated, or too tired to think things through completely. If the board's negotiator presses long enough and hard enough, she likely ends up with more than would have otherwise been the case.

The best thing for the board is that the teachers cannot just walk out. At any point, the specific issue on the table is not a deal breaker. If the teachers walk out, the board probably calls a press conference and tells the world that the teachers broke off negotiations over a minor issue. "They must not want to work this out. The board is only concerned about the welfare of the children and cannot understand where the teachers' priorities are." Also, keep in mind that whoever walks out is in a one-down position and is, to some extent, seen as the unreasonable bad guy.

The key here for the skilled manager is to keep the negotiating process in perspective. A variant of the above technique is used by players who want to rush the negotiating process. These players push to handle things quickly and casually. You hear them saying things like, "Let's go ahead and sign off on this now. We can work out the details later. We all understand what the deal is here." This "rush it through" technique usually comes up near the end of the negotiating process when people are tired and becoming impatient. The skilled manager needs only to understand a few facts of negotiating life to avoid being either worn out or rushed.

- Negotiations always take at least twice as long as planned

- Limit the length of any session ahead of time or it will likely go to the point of exhaustion

- Eighty percent of the real movement will come in the last 20 percent of the process and 15 percent will come in the last 5 percent

- The closer you are to closure, the more alert and sharp you need to be

- Take care not to get ambushed at the finish line

Players expect to get more than they give

This technique is second nature to many players and to most people. People go into negotiations with winning in mind. It may be that it is the American way—getting the best end of the deal.

With the teachers and school board, the usual assumption is that the teachers are trying to get as much as possible without taking on any additional requirements. From the other point of view, the usual assumption is that the board is trying to get more control. It wants to impose additional requirements at the least possible increase in cost. In this environment, each side has the goal of getting the other side to reduce its demands without having to increase what it gives. Success is getting as much as possible for as little as possible. The goal is to get a *good deal*.

What if one side does not press to win the negotiation? The teachers' negotiator comes close to breaking out of the traditional mold with, "We will agree to anything reasonable in these areas. We are ready to agree today. . . ."

Suppose that he takes an additional step. "Our priority is to be sure the board is completely comfortable with the final agreement. We need as much improvement for the teachers as can be worked out, but this is not our priority. We share the welfare of the children as a goal with the board and do not want to do anything to jeopardize the board's capacity in this area. The need, from the teachers' point of view, is to maximize the outcome for the board, for the teachers, and for the children. How can the teachers assure that the board is fully satisfied, comfortable with any agreement we make?"

As an experienced player, the board's negotiator will resist any efforts to move the process in this direction. Her response is, "Give us a break! The board wants to get the best range of services and mix of teachers it can get for the dollars available. The teachers want to get the best working environment and compensation package they can get. Let's not play word games with each other."

She keeps the game in the board's court, following the board's definition of successful negotiations. The issue is and will remain one of how much each side gets and how little it will have to give.

For the skilled manager, the goal is not to win. Rather, it is to assure that you receive the maximum value consistent with the consideration given. You, of course, do not want to give more than you get, but neither do you want to get more than you give. The constant question for you needs to be, "Is the other party getting as good a deal as I am?" Conversely, "Am I getting a similarly good deal?"

Along with being the right thing to do, this approach is in your simple self-interest. If you give too much and get too little, it may seem expedient but will not set well with you over time. Also, it only encourages the other party to push for an even better deal next time.

If you get too much and give too little, the outcome is reversed. The other party will resent it and will be much less willing to do business with you tomorrow. Being sure you both get equally good deals is your best way to assure future business, to foster productive relationships, and to safeguard your reputation.

Players give the impression they are giving away the store

On the surface, this technique seems like an ineffective ploy. It boils down to seeming to give away too much while not getting enough. But the skilled player makes it work to his advantage.

To understand the deception, you must first understand the standard negotiating rule. The rule says to set upper and lower limits before going into the negotiating session. The upper limit is the most that will be given away and the lower limit is the least you must get. You do not go over the upper limit or under the lower limit in the session. If necessary, you try for another session or pass up the deal before violating the rule. This is what most people understand is meant when someone says, "That is my bottom line."

Eric Grossman is a contractor who is trying to get a contract to build a small office building for a regional magazine. He and the potential lessee are in agreement on the plans for the building and have settled on everything except the monthly payments.

After about an hour of discussions, Eric says, "I just cannot make this work for $3,000 a month. It will take at least $3,600; and even then, I will just break even. At $3,000, I will be losing money. It just won't work."

The magazine's CEO is noticeably disappointed. She says, "We have gone up from $2,400. We also have lowered our space requirements more than works real well for us. We run a financially tight operation anyway and $3,000 puts us a little out on a limb. I guess it is close but no cigar."

Both parties have reached their bottom lines. You may think that they might as well shake hands and call it a day.

That is what is happening when Eric says, "This is a shame. I just hate this. There has to be some way to make this work for you. I just feel awful about this."

He is in the doorway when he turns and says, "This has to work. I have an idea. It is just an idea. I can use the tax loss for a couple of years, if you can come up a little over the years of the lease. My accountant won't speak to me for a year. [Note the good guy, bad guy ploy.] I have to make this work for you."

Does that tug your heartstrings or what? Eric is willing to lose money just to make it work. It probably comes from his charitable nature. At a minimum, he is about to give away the store. It is a wonder an altruistic player like Eric did not go broke years ago.

The management of these players is simple. If the deal seems too good to be true, or if a deal about to go sour suddenly revives, something is rotten in Denmark—as the bard cautions.

As a skilled manager, you know that if the deal is too good, you:

- Do not understand what you are actually getting

- Do not understand the true value of what you are getting, or

- Do not understand how much you are giving or its value

If the deal suddenly revives, it is easier to know exactly what is going on. The other party is being dishonest with you. They tried to make you think that you had received their best offer when it was not true. Their attempt was to pressure you into an agreement. When that strategy did not succeed, they went for the next round. They do not want to work out an agreement that benefits both of you equally. They want to win. Continue the negotiation if it is in your interest, but be careful and maintain a healthy level of skepticism.

In the example, it might be fun to resume the negotiation with Eric by saying, "Thank you for trying. I would never want to put you into that kind of position. You pay your accountant for good advice. It is probably best to follow it. Either we both get equally good deals, or I will need to pass. That is the only way I do business. It has to work well for both of us. Will what you are suggesting work well for you? Would that be a comfortable arrangement? If so, we can discuss it."

Just keep in mind that people seldom give away the store; but should they try, the skilled manager declines their suspect offer.

Players do not assume any responsibility
for assuring the other party gets a good deal

This is a hit-and-run technique best suited to players who specialize in onetime sales and services. In that context, it is an effective way of maximizing profits and minimizing the expenditure of resources. The trick is to avoid its use with regular customers or anyone who might talk to a potential customer.

A nationally known law firm is doing some work for the CIL Corporation. Through its work, it is aware of some management/organizational problems within the CIL Corp. Through inside contacts and as a result of several meetings, the law firm develops a $125,000 contract for management consultation to the corporation. The contract is loose and talks mostly about the consultation process and the fees for specific activities and reports. The contract does not specifically address the outcome of the consultation. Keep in mind that the law firm writes the contract and provides the services.

The outcome is that the corporation is totally disrupted, and many normal procedures are changed. In addition, several people within the corporation are singled out as the basis of the internal problems.

The consultants come to the conclusion that the difficulties can be reduced to two points: First, some procedures need to be changed and others need to be tightened up. Second, the CIL Corp. is told that it has a personnel problem. The final report of the consultants goes on for a hundred pages to say no more than this.

Going in, the corporation knows that it has a lot of internal squabbling and tension, and that some of its procedures need to be changed. For $125,000 the law firm verifies these perceptions.

The consultants are asked for recommendations about the personnel problems and written examples of better procedures. They say, "It is not part of the consultant's role to become involved in the day-to-day operations of your company. Our role is to give you an overview of the problems and to help define the issues. We have done this in accord with our contract. If you do not choose to use our report or do not have the expertise to use it effectively, that is not our responsibility."

The law firm takes its money and runs, leaving the CIL Corp. in a worse condition than it was before receiving the consultation services. Can you hear the consultants talking with each other?

"That company is in a mess. It is no wonder, the way they throw around their money. They thought they could spend $125,000 and fix their problems. I thought that was what they were expecting when they signed the contract. Getting into things when they don't know what they are doing is the biggest part of their problems. Oh well, business is business."

There is only one message here for you. Along with giving your customers what they request, it is also important to give them what they need. If you do not understand what is really needed from your customer's point of view, this will not be possible. Perhaps the first question should be, "What do you expect to achieve through these negotiations? What are your interests, your real needs?"

Your last question is, "Does this do the job for you? Let's talk about that in terms of what your interests and real needs were going in. This is not a onetime thing. I do not do business that way. May we spend a few minutes to be sure I am getting the job done for you?"

Postscript

Do you ever have to work with people who absolutely, totally, and unequivocally drive you up the wall? Do you sometimes feel like climbing the wall all by yourself as the quickest way to escape from those people?

You no longer have to answer **Yes! Yes! Yes!** when asked these questions. You now understand that players are primarily motivated by personal needs, status goals, insecurities, and a craving for power. They are masters at diverting attention from themselves and from their roles in the negative outcomes they cause. But no more, at least not with you.

B-t-B players will continue driving people up the wall by putting most of their time and energy into keeping things the same and avoiding responsibility; but you do not play any more. You understand that they do not trust themselves and believe any errors or mistakes will likely lead to problems for them. Instead of letting them drive you up the wall, you will emphasize positive outcomes. Although you may occasionally need to use negative reinforcement, your main approach is to teach and encourage in positive and supportive ways. You know that the reward for these players has to come primarily through success and through their increasing exercise of judgment and initiative.

Faultfinders will still enjoy blaming and accusing people and focus mostly on what is not going well. You now see that they are not accepting of others but are not accepting of themselves either. As you watch them, you see that they treat themselves as critically as they treat others.

As a skilled counter player, you no longer come to the bait. You resist the urge to react negatively, to tell them off, to refuse to work with them, or to resign to the inevitable while you are boiling inside. You make the changes that are appropriate and reasonable. The rest of the time, you do only what needs to be done as well as it needs doing. Additionally, you find honest opportunities to say supportive things to these players. You point out what they have done especially well and comment favorably when one of their skills or abilities makes things easier or helps things turn out successfully.

Warriors will continue to be ready to go to war over anything and try to take charge of everything and everyone. You know that they are overly aggressive, insensitive, rigid, and have an unusual need to control people and situations. At the same time, you see that they mistrust everyone and their motives. They operate mostly out of fear and insecurity and honestly believe keeping absolute control is the only way to be safe. Their game is and will remain a matter of who has the most muscle and the greatest willingness to go to the mat over everything.

As a skilled counter player, your strategy is not to be intimidated and to never come to the bait, no matter how tempting or irresistible. The bait, of course, is the urge to defend yourself, attack the warrior, become totally frustrated, and either quit or simply capitulate to his will.

Bummed out players will still pursue their energy draining games. They are negative about everything and do not deal well with the ups and downs of organizational life. You see that they use the technique to avoid responsibility, to get others to back off, and to avoid work or pressure.

As a skilled counter player, you simply outwait them. You bring up a problem or issue and then wait for a response other than the bummed out replies you have heard before. You respond only to positive and productive behavior and organize the work so such behavior is expected and required.

Committee players will be as creative as ever at finding excuses for not getting the job done and as busy as ever at avoiding making decisions. You now understand that their motivations are in their desire to get special concessions, preferential treatment, or exemption from responsibilities. You no longer go along with their behavior and refuse to accept their excuses. You set the same standard for action and participation for them as you hold for everyone else. When a player does not come up to your standard, you call him on it, making it clear to him and others that his committee game will not work with you.

Mainliners will persist with their strategy of trying to solve problems without knowing why the problems came up in the first place, starting jobs without knowing what you expect, and getting involved in tasks that they neither understand nor know how to do. You now understand the simple fact that these players do not know how to do the job needing to be done and would rather foul everything up than admit the truth. Their only goal is to avoid being found out, to bluff their way through, no matter what the cost.

As an effective counter player, you do not accept excuses and explanations that are not factual or do not have a ring of truth. If things are getting worse, if problems are getting out of hand, if business is going down the tube, you know that the likelihood is that you have a mainliner at work. You set specific criteria for deciding if things are moving toward or away from the goal. If there is no movement toward the goal or especially if there is movement away from it, you hold the player accountable. You listen to the excuses and explanations and then hold him responsible.

I-players will continue to consider only their simple self-interest and have little concern about the motivations and interests of others. You know that these players truly believe their skills and abilities are better than they are. Even though they are competent at some things, they usually perceive themselves as being the best at whatever it is. They also believe that everyone else, including you, is much less competent than they are.

Now that you are a serious counter player, you are consciously and intentionally self-assured, assertive, and persistent with these players. You know that being fair, firm, and consistent is usually enough. If not, you are ready, though. Among your additional strategies is simply "calling" these players, to use an old poker play. A player thinks he is the most knowledgeable, the most effective, the best, and believes he can handle anything. Whenever he says there is a problem, you call him on it. You confidently say, "Given your skills and experience, you are the logical choice to handle this. Please take care of it." It is "put up or shut up" time.

Impersonal players will still not understand the needs of others, will not think people need reasons or explanations, and will not have much understanding of their roles with others. Nonetheless, you are certainly up to the challenge. You know that these players are either incapable of or unwilling to think about things in human terms. They attempt to handle everything and everyone in impersonal ways.

This is not a problem for you anymore. Since they are know-it-alls and do not think they have to come down to the people level—an idea that they do not understand anyway—you stay as calm and as rational as possible. You give the impression of not caring about things in any feeling or emotional ways. Instead, you convey a dispassionate but committed approach to the issues. You are a machine responding to another machine.

Agitators will continue to get others upset and then act innocent, make things seem worse than they are, have opinions on everything, and keep things stirred up. However, you are now a counter player who understands that these players will say anything no matter who gets hurt or feels badly. They do it for a cheap moment in the spotlight, to get attention, to get a little more power for awhile, to be seen as in the know, and to be on top of things. You also do not forget that they will say anything about anyone, including you.

Counter play now becomes easy for you. You say, "You are a trip. You can find more ways to look at things negatively than anyone I know." In another situation, you may say, "I am surprised to hear you say that. I do not think it is true." If all else fails, you might say, "You probably would describe the tooth fairy as a thief." Whatever your response, you make your point and let it go. You are the one who decides when enough is enough.

A FINAL THOUGHT

Most people are honest, forthright, and sincerely trying to work with you in positive and constructive ways. They come to work wanting to contribute to the success of your business and believing that they can and will make a positive difference. Although they may inadvertently slip into behavior like that seen in players, they are not players. They are quality people who sometimes are not at their best. These people need and deserve your patience, understanding, sensitivity, and support. As a good manager, you need to cut them a little slack from time to time, give them the benefit of the doubt, and avoid finger pointing and name calling. They truly are your most important assets and the keys to your success.

Among the many, there are the few, nonetheless. The players of the world are alive and well and ready to drive you up the wall if you let them. That is the conclusion to take to heart. Players will play anywhere, anytime, with anyone who will play. That is what they do. The issue for you is whether you will play their games.

If "up the wall" is not for you and if your frustration factor needs some serious attention, you are ready for counter play. You are now familiar with the techniques and strategies of effective counter players and have only to incorporate them into your managerial repertoire. But there is one final technique that you need to know to round out your counter play.

Pursue your counter play as you do everything else you do—with style, all the time, and on purpose. For you, counter play cannot be a casual activity or something done occasionally. It must be integral to you and a matter of professional pride.